The Unexpected Adventure of Growing Old

Leah Friedman

Life brings us two gifts: a moment in time, and the consciousness of its brevity. We owe life two things in return: a life fully lived, and the gift surrendered at the end. But consider also that how we view this journey is profoundly influenced by the lens through which we see the world.

James Hollis
On This Journey We Call Our Life

For information contact CroneLeah@aol.com

Library of Congress Cataloging-in-Publication Data

The Unexpected Adventure of Growing Old
Leah Friedman

ISBN-13: 978-0692859698
ISBN-10: 0692859691

Cover design and interior by Paul E. Jost
Cover image: Leah Friedman

The typeface used in this book is Minion®, a 1990 Adobe Originals typeface by Robert Slimbach. Minion is inspired by classical, old-style typefaces of the late Renaissance, a period of elegant, beautiful, and highly readable type designs.

Table of Contents

Dedication

To all those, young and old, who seek how best to live a good life up to the very end.

~

Acknowledgements

I am deeply indebted to Sara Jenkins, who has offered not only her skills as editor but also given unstinting support as a friend throughout the process of writing this book. Her guidance and encouragement kept me going even when I was ready to abandon the project. So, thank you, Sara!

I also thank Anna Navarro and Suzanne Doyle for reading early versions of the manuscript and offering helpful suggestions. Their feedback is greatly appreciated.

Paul E. Jost designed the cover and text of the book, for which I am most grateful. He is a delight to work with.

Lest there be any doubt, all errors or misrepresentations are solely my responsibility.

Introduction

Now in my eighty-eighth year, I have been reflecting on exactly how I got to be who I am. I find it to be a great mystery. My identity was determined in certain ways by my genetic heritage, then shaped by the circumstances of my growing up, my family and the rural Southern culture of that time. Those early years are often considered the most formative, and certainly they contributed in large measure to my fundamental psychic structure. Nevertheless, at this late stage of my life those influences seem to fade in significance compared with the experiences I have had and the relationships I have formed in the decades since I turned sixty. I find these later years have unquestionably had an important determining effect on who I have become.

This book began with my curiosity about that process and a questioning of attitudes that characterize aging as a time of deprivation rather than a time of enrichment. Growing old is a normal progression, experienced by all of us who are lucky enough to live a long life. All too frequently, however, the very idea of becoming old, as predictable as it is, fills us with apprehension. Picturing ourselves as sick, disabled, and dependent on others, we tend to dread this stage of life. But I am drawn to a very different view of aging, suggested by T. S. Eliot when he says *Old men ought to be explorers*. As an old woman I look back on my life in the past few decades as a fascinating exploration of unknown territory.

As aging explorers we will encounter unexpected terrain and confront seemingly insurmountable obstacles—bewildering wilderness, valleys of sorrow, towering mountains, and dangerous waters. But if we enter this territory of old age with a spirit of adventure, we may also stumble upon stunning landscapes, move up from the depths, attain unforeseen heights of joy, and sail through deeply satisfying placid seas. As with any demanding undertaking, growing old requires resilience, endurance, and acceptance of whatever difficulties we must face along the way.

Just as children's growth requires learning new skills to adapt to their changing bodies and minds, so it is with growing old. When young we benefited from being playful, creative, open to adventure, and receptive to new ideas. As we age these same qualities can support our journey into a new stage of life. By embracing our aging, adjusting to its alterations, and focusing on the advantages it can bring, we may transform ourselves in the process. Indeed, the knowledge that our time is drawing short offers unparalleled opportunities to strengthen our character and deepen our emotional and spiritual outlook.

I am fortunate to remain in overall good health, which has considerable bearing on my positive, though realistic, approach to aging. But physical well-being alone does not determine our approach to aging and death. More important is our ability to find meaning in these late years, through the rewarding process of becoming conscious of and grateful for the lessons that life has offered us.

The past century has seen an astonishing rise in life expectancy. Reportedly, two-thirds of all persons who have reached age sixty-five are now alive; reaching ages eighty or ninety is no longer the anomaly it once was. Those of us who are elders have more political influence, greater wealth, and more vitality than any generation before us. By shifting our perspective and focusing on more of the affirmative aspects of aging, by resolving to live life to its fullest as long as we are alive, we can not only reap the considerable rewards of our longevity but also challenge the disparaging stereotypes of the elderly so prevalent in our society.

My interest has been to examine varied aspects of aging, through what I have learned from the writings and observations of others and what I have experienced in my almost nine decades of life. Though I have chosen a particular order, these chapters may be read randomly, as essays. I hope that readers will sense between the lines how I share the sentiment expressed by the ancient Roman philosopher Cicero, who wrote about aging: "For me, writing this book has been so delightful that it has not only erased all the petty annoyances of old age but has also made old age soft and pleasant."

$\sim$

Cicero, Marcus Tullius. *An Essay on Old Age*. 44 BC. Trans. W. Melmoth. Google ebook.

Eliot, T. S. "Four Quartets," *Collected Poems 1909-1962*. New York: Harcourt Brace Jovanovich, 1991.

Launching the Adventure: Aging and Ageism

The typical stereotypes of ageism suggest that people over age 65 are all sick and frail or worse: impoverished, impotent, senile, and unhappy.

Harry R. Moody
Aging: Concepts and Controversies

That Word "Old"

When we embark on a journey or launch a new venture, we expect to confront a few impediments along the way. In the case of transforming our notion of aging, we need to acknowledge one major hurdle, and that is the pervasiveness of ageism. Ageism is defined as prejudice or discrimination against a particular age group, especially the elderly. It involves stereotyping and holding negative views of old people, biases frequently found in our youth-oriented society. Our ability to retain a sense of self-worth into our old age depends in large part on our acceptance and understanding of this period of our lives as having its own meaning and value; nevertheless, we must contend with the attitudes of the culture which surrounds us, attitudes that can be hurtful and damaging due to overt hostility or a subtler antipathy towards those of us who are old.

It puzzles me (and, I must admit, annoys me) that so many people are reluctant to use the word *old*. In a conversation with a friend when I was eighty, I referred to myself as an old woman, an age that by anyone's measure is considered old. She admonished me: "It seemed strange to hear you put yourself in the category of old woman. I think of you as young, sharp as a tack, and with it." While her response was flattering, I could not help but wonder why she considered the term "old woman" pejorative rather than merely descriptive. Had I spoken of a "young woman," surely there would have been no cause for comment, no value judgment placed on the term. Why is being an old woman (or old man) something to be ashamed of? Can I not be "old, sharp as a tack, and with it"? Must I be embarrassed about claiming the lessons I have learned, the activities I have enjoyed, the relationships I have cherished, the life I have lived? Why should I not be proud of my years, proud of being old?

Others have similar complaints. Susan Moon, a Zen Buddhist writing about getting old, has this observation about those who say to old people, "Even if you're old, you can still be young at heart!" She points out that there is in this statement an assumption that old is bad and young is good—a fairly common assumption in my experience. She exclaims, "What's wrong with being 'old at heart,' I'd like to know? 'Old at heart'— doesn't it have a beautiful ring? Wouldn't you like to be loved by people whose hearts have practiced loving for a long time?" I say, yes, we of the old must somehow reclaim our status as humans who have benefited from our years upon this earth, who refuse to deny our age, who proclaim our significance to society, and who are satisfied, even delighted, in being old, and most certainly old at heart.

Unfortunately, for many people, applying the word *old* to a friend or acquaintance of advanced age arouses the fear of being judgmental or even insulting. It is as if the term *old*—truthful though it may be—is tainted by some distinctly unpleasant odor. Perhaps it is a lost cause, but I wish to reclaim the word, scrub it clean of such misplaced pollution, reclaim its dignity, integrity, and honesty, and replace its smell of denigration with a more neutral scent, or better still, allow it the sweet fragrance of well-earned deference. Perhaps we could then help shift the word *old* from meaning something vaguely offensive to something respectable or perhaps even admirable. There is, after all, something to admire in those of us who have reached advanced age—if for nothing else because we have survived the challenges of a long life.

The disrespect that accompanies ageism, however unconscious, is revealed in a variety of ways. I am sure many of us old people have been approached by well-meaning salespersons who in a cloying, patronizing tone, say, "May I help you, young woman (or man)?" When this happens to me I bristle, wishing I could recite to the offending individual a poem titled "Don't Call Me a Young Woman" by Ruth Harriet Jacobs, who was born in 1924 and died in 2013 at age eighty-eight. She was a poet, gerontologist, sociologist, researcher at Wellesley College, and author of nine books, including *Be An Outrageous Older Woman*. She expresses my feelings about these encounters:

> Don't call me a young woman.
> I was a young woman for years
> but that was then and this is now.
> I was a mid life woman for a time
> and I celebrated that good span.
> Now I am somebody magnificent, new,
> a seer, wise woman, old proud crone,
> an example and mentor to the young
> who need to learn old women wisdom.
> I look back on jobs well done
> And learn to do different tasks now.
> I think great thoughts and share them.
>
> Don't call me a young woman.
> You reveal your own fears of aging.
> Maybe you'd better come learn from
> all of us wonderful old women
> how to take the sum of your life
> with all its experience and knowledge
> and show how a fully developed life

can know the joy of a past well done
and the joy of life left to live.

Don't call me a young woman;
it's not a compliment or courtesy
but rather a grating discourtesy.
Being old is a hard won achievement
not something to be brushed aside
treated as infirmity or ugliness
or apologized away by "young woman."
I am an old woman, a long liver,
I'm proud of it. I revel in it.
I wear my grey hair and wrinkles
as badges of triumphant survival
and I intend to grow even older.

Jacobs's observation that such people are projecting their own fears of growing old onto others seems reasonable, for all of us know something of that fear. Some of us, even if we ourselves are already past middle age, often harbor unconscious disparaging thoughts regarding aging; we have been conditioned by our cultural environment to view old age as disagreeable, deplorable, dreaded, to be avoided if possible, though I would argue that the alternative—never being old—is certainly not more enticing. I urge those of us in our sixties, seventies, eighties, and beyond, to not only insist on being treated with respect, but also to honestly and forthrightly acknowledge our status as being *old*. If we own the word and use it with pride, then perhaps others will adopt our usage and thereby help shed it of its negative connotations. There is no shame in having lived a long life.

Age and Appearance

One of the most obvious signs of ageism is our obsession with physical appearance. According to the prevalent standards of our culture, we are supposed to always look fresh, unblemished—young!—so we search for any possible means to delay the evidence of encroaching age. While we wish to continue adding years to our lives, we suffer the illusion that if only we erase our wrinkles, banish our baldness, color our hair, liposuction away our fat, then perhaps we can fool ourselves and our bodies into believing we are still young. All this emphasis on resisting aging has as its underlying message that being old, or more specifically, looking old, is definitely not desirable. Such views and fears contribute to attitudes of ageism.

Our current media are dominated by advertisements for anti-aging products. We are given hollow promises and false hopes from an industry that profits by inciting fear and exploiting our insecurities. As many persons have pointed out, the only certain method of wrinkle prevention is death at a young age. When we are told to remove our blemishes we are being asked to delete much that we have spent a lifetime creating. By trying to eradicate our wrinkles and lift our facial contours we are attempting to wipe away the evidence of all we have learned, all we have suffered, and all we have loved. And it is certain that we are not given youth in return. It is a tragic illusion. Our age remains the same.

The use of hair color and anti-wrinkle skin lotions is minor and painless compared with other more drastic methods used to ward off the effects of aging. Not only are Botox treatments readily available and widely used to smooth out folds in the face, but cosmetic surgeries, such as facelifts, eye-lifts, tummy tucks, and liposuction are also becoming more frequently utilized as a means of denying our stage of life. These procedures are tolerated in an effort to remove signs of the undeniable fact of our vanishing youthfulness.

It is quite possible that a facelift can sometimes give a (temporary) boost to a woman's (or a man's) flagging spirits by removing a few wrinkles, but the oft-repeated facial surgery of some public (and private) figures has stretched the skin so tight that they look more like marble statues than living beings. Their glassy-smooth countenances have none of the crinkly eyes and jiggling jowls that result from genuine laughter or the sagging muscles reflecting heavy responsibilities or the weight of grief, or simply the downward pull of gravity over many years. Altering one's facial configuration in a misplaced desire to appear forever young is not only futile but distressing, for these tragic, inert, fixed visages offer no verification of fully lived lives and therefore fail to express the full extent of their human proficiencies and potential. I much prefer to have my face reflect the range of my experiences, sad and happy, heartbreaking and heart-filling, that I have been privileged to endure.

It is heartening to know that many of us—even famous figures—do not fall prey to these false inducements. The author M. F. K. Fisher wrote shortly before her death that she knows "some women who refuse to be old and they are like zombies walking around. They are lifted here and lifted there; you know, altered in the nose and eyes and chin, and they can't smile because it would ruin their latest do…. It's okay if they feel better, but I think they are compromising their fate and I refuse to do that. That's all, I refuse." Her refusal offers a healthy perspective for those of us who wish to embrace our aging faces and bodies.

Another woman with a constructive, upbeat approach to aging and a resistance to ageism was legendary performer Eartha Kitt, who in the year before her eightieth birthday was featured in an off-Broadway musical, appeared at Café Carlyle in New York City, and released an album of live songs, as well as appearing at the White House—all while being treated for colon cancer. Before her death in 2008 she was quoted as saying, "Aging is a natural process, so enjoy it." She added that she had never resorted to anything other than exercising, eating right, and keeping a positive attitude in order to look good. "I don't believe in chopping up my face in order to look like something I might have looked like when I was thirty." Would that we all could follow her example and accept aging as the natural process it is.

A recent comment on the frequent use of Botox comes from Jennifer Aniston who is quoted as saying, "I think what I have been witness to, is seeing women [in Hollywood] trying to stay ageless with what they are doing to themselves. I am grateful to learn from their mistakes, because I am not injecting shit into my face.… I see them and my heart breaks.… They are trying to stop the clock and all you can see is an insecure person who won't let themselves just age." In my view, her remarks reflect a more enlightened view from one of the younger stars of movies and television.

Barbara Macdonald and Cynthia Rich, in their courageous little book, *Look Me in the Eye*, comment on the attitudes toward aging they see around them, noting how much women fear the stigma of age and how little is understood about this reality in our lives. Macdonald writes with startling honesty about her aging body. Not only does she have gray hair and a deeply lined face, she also writes about seeing the loose skin on her forearm and hardly believing it is really her own. In spite of these startling changes, Macdonald declares, "The truth is I like growing old."

Another woman, Virginia Ironside, in her semi-autobiographical book about aging, has her character Marie make similar observations: "The backs of my hands are speckled with brown spots. When did they appear? Only a few years ago, I think, when I could pretend to myself (talk about denial!) that I was about thirty. Now, my entire body is shrieking at me that I am old. And what's so utterly strange is that I don't really mind a bit. It feels rather comfortable, friendly—and right."

I have resisted most efforts to deny the effects of aging. Coloring my hair always seemed too much trouble, so it is now completely gray. My skin is rough, flaky, and mottled from too much sun exposure when I was young. Like Macdonald and her arms, I have a similar sense of amazement when I look at my hands, covered with splotchy brown spots and bulging veins, and my fingers, gnarled and swollen from arthritis. I am not ashamed of my hands, for they have served me well through the years of my life. Embracing my appearance—whatever it is—without apology or regret adds to my joy and satisfaction with life. I too like growing old; the changes feel just right, appropriate for my age.

To make a point about affirming my aging, I decided some time ago, in my curmudgeonly way, to refuse to say "thank you" when on occasion someone tells me I look younger than my age. I feel that to accept such a remark as flattering only reinforces the inescapable implication that it is not a good thing to look old, even if that is what I truly am. I am tempted to say (following the example of Gloria Steinem), "But this is how eighty-eight looks!" On the other hand, it is undoubtedly true that we age in different ways and at different rates. It is a challenge to remain gracious and at the same time let others know that I am realistic and unapologetic about just where I am in the cycle of my life.

It is important to acknowledge that there is nothing wrong with looking good. In fact, there is a measure of self-esteem apparent when we pay attention to our appearance. It is commendable to see old women who have cultivated their own kind of dress, who are no longer slaves to the latest fashion but have found clothing that provides both comfort and style suitable for their stage of life. The sad thing is that so few designers are interested in creating apparel for those of us in our later years. Most are focused on the tastes of the young.

François Mauriac made an interesting comparison between the stages of life and weather conditions which seems pertinent to this discussion regarding growing old. He says, "What I called mild weather and which I so highly prized in former times I can now easily do without, having reached the age of contemplation.... Fine weather is a prejudice of youth. For an old man, the weather can be neither fine nor bad; it is the very texture of the weather that seems priceless, whether brightened by shafts of sunlight or clouded with darkness." Similarly, it is our complex, intriguing texture, including wrinkles and folds, blotches and spots, woven into our faces and our bodies throughout the years, that, when viewed from a point of view that values aging, can create a special appeal. These visible features suggest that we have endured all kinds of weather and that our physical form, whatever our age, is a part of our fundamental essence.

Ageism, with its focus on outward appearance, affects women most of all, though increasingly men are being seduced by the desire to look as youthful as possible and are resorting to facelifts. Though there are many old men still in prominent positions, we do not hear much talk of how they look or what they wear. Women in the public arena, on the other hand, are carefully scrutinized and often criticized for failures of fashion or figure or for facial flaws. One cannot escape the regrettable notion that sexism as well as ageism is still widely practiced.

Invisibility

Ironically, along with being the primary targets of the marketing of anti-aging products, women are especially prone to becoming invisible as we grow old. Many of us have been in social groups where young people have difficulty making eye contact. They look through us and over us, but not *at* us. We stand in a business establishment and watch as younger customers are seen and approached while we are disregarded. There has developed among many of our fellow humans a blind spot, a failure to bring into view those of us who do not fit into their vision of youthful worthiness. This can be infuriating; we resent being overlooked as much as we as we dislike being patronized.

This not-being-seen Moon calls "the invisibility factor." She says that gray hair shrouds us in a fog, making it necessary for us to proclaim our presence. She feels that facelifts might be less an act of "counterfeiting" than an effort "to tear away the veil that society projects onto our faces." She goes on to say that "it's not the wrinkles themselves that hurt, it's the meaning they are given, a meaning that is mostly unconscious and unspoken." We cannot help but feel demeaned when we are deliberately snubbed or ignored.

As insulting or disturbing as it is not to be seen, on occasion we might find some advantages in fading from view. Often our age allows us relief from having to conform to conventional behavior and appearance standards. The freedom is that of throwing off old restraints and old patterns; no longer shackled by fear of rejection and need for acceptance, we can act out our impulses, be outrageous, be ourselves. If we wish, we can dress unfashionably and comfortably, confident that we will not be scrutinized—but can still enjoy studying those around us. As octogenarian Penelope Lively puts it, "We are not exactly invisible, but we are not noticed, which I rather like; it leaves me free to... listen and watch...as though I am some observant time-traveler, on the edge of things, bearing witness to the customs of another age."

For those of us in the older generation these observations can at times tend towards being judgmental; for example, I cannot understand the need for youngsters to constantly peer at their cell phones, endlessly tweeting and texting. But the broader perspective we have on current styles and customs is helpful, for we understand that change in cultural patterns is inevitable. Our very invisibility as elders gives us a protected position from which we can be more accepting of passing fads and political upheavals, for we have witnessed many in our time.

Another aspect of ageism that contributes to our invisibility is that we suffer from being stereotyped. All too often we are seen as anonymous members of a group, all of whom are considered to be basically alike— "old," no longer "with it," thought to be "over the hill." But that certainly is not the case. In spite of this frequent misperception, the fact is that we become more heterogeneous as we age. We are creatures with different histories, personalities, abilities, and complexities. Our attitudes towards life and aging vary according to our gender, our social class, our ethnicity, and our personal history. We feel aggrieved when we are placed in a category that does not allow for our fundamental individuality. We dislike being pigeonholed. We deserve to be recognized as unique persons.

Confronting Ageism

In combatting ageism it will be necessary to change our attitude toward, and our expectations of, aging. Partly this depends on where we place our focus. In his study of old age the archetypal psychologist James Hillman writes, "As long as we regard each tremor, each little liver spot, each forgotten name as only a sign of decay, we are afflicting older age with our minds as much as our minds are afflicted by older age." He goes on to say that it isn't just our knees and hips that need replacement, it is our ideas of old age that must be replaced. As he succinctly puts it, "The main pathology of later years is our idea of later years." It is essential, therefore, that we discard those outmoded and harmful ideas and that we begin to think in terms that will boost our spirits and broaden our understanding of what aging is all about.

For one thing, perhaps we need to acknowledge a variety of types of beauty. Just as there is the soft, sweet loveliness of the dawn, the strong, invigorating magnificence of the noonday sun, and the fading splendor of the sunset, so might we broaden our view to see attractive qualities at all stages of life. The young are certainly exquisite in their freshness and innocence; the middle-aged may display focus and vigor; but many old people are equally dazzling due to an appealing glow of the life force that continues to enliven their beings.

Maybe it is because I am old myself that I have come to admire the special radiance of the aged. I know women in their eighties and nineties whom I consider to be absolutely stunning. Their hair is silver, their wrinkled faces shine with warmth and openness, their eyes twinkle with humor, their bodies are rounded and soft, and they carry themselves—often slowly—with stateliness, poise, and grace. That particular kind of presence only comes with age. Unfortunately, in our culture of youth, it is often overlooked and undervalued.

Though I frequently see beauty in those of advanced age, it is the blemishes, scars, wrinkles, age spots, drooping skin, and sagging bodies accompanied by the loving gaze, open heart, welcoming arms, and hearty laughter that make us who we are. All are the result of embracing our lives fully regardless of age. To deny the flaws is to obliterate the experiences and exposures that have created not just the wrinkles in our faces, but also the strengths in our personalities. Those very markings are a product of our life's adventures; they constitute an essential part of our being, and they feel right.

Successful Aging

If we are not to be judged by the standards of the young, just what does it mean to age successfully? The conventional view in our extraverted, action-oriented society is to think of success in aging as the ability to continue to function as we did in middle age. We admire those who remain healthy and vigorous, who are fortunate enough to be without debilitating illness or disability. By adopting that stance, we are applying the standards of midlife to old age, suggesting that those who maintain more youthful levels of activity are therefore "successful." But that attitude fails to recognize that aging has its own pace, its own style, and its own constraints. As Jungian analyst Lionel Corbett says, "[S]uccessful aging refers to a person's perceived satisfaction with his or her ability to adapt to physical and functional changes over time, while maintaining connection to others, interdependence and a sense of meaning and purpose in life." When we reach our seventies, eighties and nineties, we are in a decidedly different stage of life and therefore must adjust to a different set of standards. To deny the significance of the shift can be another form of ageism.

Recently I was invited to participate in a panel of "Successful Agers." We were all in reasonably good health and engaged in a variety of endeavors. One woman in her nineties is still painting, another also in her tenth decade teaches ballet to children, yet another is involved in community art projects. The men on the panel participate in comparable pursuits, contributing their energy and experience in business and civic affairs to their communities. While these activities are certainly worthy of respect, there are other elders, confined to wheelchairs or otherwise incapacitated, who are facing their late years with enormous toughness, courage, and determination, and they too are successful agers. If we can maintain our resilience, hold on to our sense of humor, and continue to find meaning and purpose in our lives, then I would say that we are living a successful old age regardless of physical condition.

Dr. George E. Vaillant, director of the Landmark Harvard Study of Adult Development, addresses what he calls successful aging and equates that with *joy*. As he puts it, "The heart speaks with so much more vitality than the head." He points out that though old age can be both miserable and joyous, our outlook depends on which facets we choose to dwell upon. His research shows that the elders who are most successful are healthy, capable of surmounting the inevitable crises of aging, and able to constantly reinvent their lives. Even in times of hardship, sorrow, or great loss they never relinquish their desire to keep on living. He says, "Positive aging means to love, to work, to learn something we did not know yesterday, and to enjoy the remaining precious moments with loved ones." Surely those who grow into this outlook deserve to be called not only successful but also wise.

I would wish that all individuals who have made it through to old age could be seen as worthy of wearing their years and their looks with pride, as was traditionally the case with other cultures. We elders have knowledge gained from our experience and valuable perspectives unknown to the young, for we can see deep into the past. We carry the stories of our families and our communities. We know who we are. We have a sense of gratitude, optimism, joy, and equanimity. Surely these are significant attributes deserving of respect, regardless of the status of our health. Not that we old people are universally admirable, charming, or wise, but we should not tolerate being denigrated because of our age.

If we expect and embrace the positive experiences of growing old, if we maintain optimism regarding what aging offers, and if we accept as natural the physical changes in our bodies and in our appearance, we may help dissolve some of the negative attitudes of ageism.

$\sim$

Aniston, Jennifer. "Jennifer Aniston Speaks Out Against Botox, Reveals An Even Larger Cultural Problem." *Huffington Post,* August 15, 2014.

Corbett, Lionel. "Successful Aging: Jungian Contributions to Development in Later Life." *Jung and Aging: Possibilities and Potentials for the Second Half of Life.* Eds. Leslie Sawin, Lionel Corbett, and Michael Carbine. New Orleans: Spring Journal Books, 2014.

Fisher, M. F. K. Interview in *The Ageless Spirit: Reflections on Living Life to the Fullest in Our Later Years.* Eds. Philip L. Berman and Connie Goldman. New York: Ballantine, 1992.

Hillman, James. *The Force of Character and the Lasting Life.* New York: Random House, 1999.

Ironside, Virginia. *No! I Don't Want to Join a Book Club: Dairy of a 60th Year.* New York: Viking, 2006.

Jacobs, Ruth Harriet. "Don't Call Me a Young Woman," in *Be an Outrageous Older Woman.* New York: Harper-Collins, 1991.

Kitt, Eartha. "Still in the Limelight, on Her Own Terms." *New York Times.* December 2, 2006.

Lively, Penelope. *Dancing Fish and Ammonites: A Memoir.* New York: Viking, 2013.

Macdonald, Barbara and Cynthia Rich. *Look Me in the Eye: Old Women, Aging and Ageism.* San Francisco, CA: Spinsters/Aunt Lute, 1983.

Mauriac, François. "Man and Nature, and Art, and What It Should Be," in *The Inner Presence: Recollections of My Spiritual Life.* Trans. Herman Briffaut. Paris: Flammarion, 1968.

Moody, Harry R. *Aging: Concepts and Controversies.* 4th ed. Thousand Oaks, CA: Sage Publications, 2002.

Moon, Susan. *This Is Getting Old: Zen Thoughts on Aging with Humor and Dignity.* Boston: Shambhala, 2010.

Vaillant, George E., M.D. *Aging Well: Surprising Guideposts to a Happier Life from the Landmark Harvard Study of Adult Development.* Boston: Little, Brown, 2002.

Sixty—What Is Happening to Me?

In the past few years, I have made a thrilling discovery...
that until one is over sixty, one can never really learn the
secret of living. One can then begin to live, not simply with
the intense part of oneself, but with one's entire being.

Ellen Glasgow
The Woman Within

The First Inkling

Something strange and new was going on, but I was not at all clear just
what it might be. In my early sixties I slowly became aware of a nebulous
but undeniable change that was taking place in my thinking, in my
emotions, and in my lifestyle. Though I faced no major problems, I was
mildly depressed and vaguely apprehensive, as if something was amiss,
or missing, or unfinished. During that time I spent a few days alone in
the country, and while there I wrote my adult daughters a letter expressing
some of my thoughts and concerns. I told them that I felt on the verge of
a psychic shift, perhaps was about to embark on an inner journey, the
purpose or destination of which I had only the haziest hints. I wrote that
I was beginning to feel a need for more solitude and that I was searching
for deeper meaning in my life.

I now realize that I was at the beginning of a series of shifts marking my
entrance into old age. Though it was a new feeling and in spite of my
uncertainty and confusion, I seemed to realize at some subconscious

level that there was more to do, more to learn, more growth possible. In retrospect I can see that I was on the cusp of an amazing, deeply satisfying, entirely unimagined period of my life. This was in the early 1990s, and I was doing a lot of reading on feminism, feminine spirituality, and Jungian psychology. I had become interested in dreams and was keeping a dream journal. I began doing rituals for myself and for my family and friends. But I had no idea where those interests of mine would lead me in the years to follow.

Only now, more than two and a half decades later, have I become fully aware of how all those interests that arose in the early stage of my aging process turned out to be so crucial in helping form the person I am today. That desire to "find deeper meaning in my life," ill-defined and tentative as it was at the time, contributed in a major way to the motivation, curiosity, and searching that made possible the transformative activities that I was to pursue in my subsequent years of aging.

The Stages of Aging

If I had had a better understanding at the time of the potentials of old age I might have been better prepared for the following years of my life course. But maybe it is always fundamentally the unfolding of life itself that is our wisest and most significant guide. It is impossible to know just what we will be up against and how we will live out our years; there are no guarantees. Nevertheless, it might be helpful to identify some of the patterns established earlier in our lives, noting which ones were advantageous, which were not, and which continue to influence our development as we grow into old age. It is also important to understand that things are not forever fixed, that we can remain resilient, still capable of resolving lingering conflicts and integrating lessons learned from new experiences. We can, by looking inward and by observing others, discover where we fit into the continuum of aging; we can note how those older than we are have adjusted to their final decades. By honestly examining our own life trajectory and those of other elders we might learn to address our aging process more hopefully and more rationally.

Unlike past generations, individuals now in their early sixties are likely to live two, three, or possibly four more decades. Given this expanse of time, even the term "old age" loses much of its meaning; it suggests too broad a category to encompass the number of years and the variety of opportunities and challenges we encounter once we have left middle age behind. I am acutely aware that the way I was in my sixties and seventies is not at all the same as I am now in my late eighties. Since we are living so much longer, it seems fitting that we view our later years as not one neatly defined stage but a series of stages, each with its own characteristics and demands.

Any such partitioning is arbitrary and must be presented with carefully considered reservations. Still, based on evidence gathered from personal experience and observation of others, it is possible to consider stages defined roughly in terms of decades. In doing so, it will be helpful to keep in mind that the age limits for these phases are far from exact, since physical and emotional changes overlap to a large extent and vary greatly from one individual to another. Some persons do not experience the sense of moving into old age until their seventies; others may recognize the signs earlier. But sooner or later all of us must acknowledge that we are moving into a new period of our lives.

Young Old Age

At age fifty we frequently are in the midst of an exciting and rewarding time of life. That mid-century mark offers an opportunity for us to celebrate many of our accomplishments: careers founded, creative projects completed, homes established, and perhaps children reaching late teenage or young adulthood. Yet there remains a substantial future to live into, with ample time and opportunity for more to be done. It is as if we stand at a summit where the vista of the past and the panorama of the future are both in full view; we can look backward with satisfaction (and maybe some regrets) while looking forward with hope and confidence.

But when the next decade rolls around, usually between sixty and sixty-five, many of us (as in my case) suddenly become aware that something profound has shifted. We are startled by the realization that we are no longer young, are not even considered middle-aged. We are often surprised at this new vision of ourselves, unaccustomed and resistant to thinking of ourselves as *old*. Because there is no clear demarcation between middle age and old age, we may slide seamlessly into our later years without even noticing that it's happening. Life is commonly experienced as a continuous stream of days, months, years, each folding into the next without any clear distinction regarding what phase we may be entering or leaving.

There comes a point when we are awakened to reality. Gone is the sense of balance between past and future that we experienced at fifty; in its place there arises an awareness that the majority of our life span is behind us. We are now passing through a portal into old age. As we enter this passage we are stepping into a new way of life, or at least inaugurating a new way of looking at our lives. It is helpful for us to acknowledge that we are on the cusp of a new stage or, more correctly, additional *stages*, of life, for then we can more readily accommodate the changes to come. It is likely that in our sixties we begin to think about the years we have remaining, and, like the objects in a rearview mirror, they may be closer than they appear.

Moving into this seventh decade can make us more aware of limits, seeing ahead a looming landscape of endings rather than beginnings: an empty household, energies waning, and opportunities receding. The decade of our sixties can be an awesome milestone or an alarming reminder that our days on this earth are numbered. We have set foot on a path that, health (and fate) permitting, leads indubitably to old age. Such a realization of impending boundaries can be a shock to our former sense of self as forever young and vital and can bring on depression, disorientation, and denial. It can arouse memories of lost opportunities, failed relationships, and misplaced priorities.

But looked at another way (again, as it was for me), our early sixties can be an entry into an expanding, exciting, and engaging period of our lives, with unanticipated opportunities and surprising experiences ahead of us. This period of being "young old," when we are still strong, vital, and involved, presents us with a chance to embrace each day with renewed commitment to live the remainder of our lives to the fullest. With many of our practical goals realized, we can mobilize our energies toward those areas of our lives previously unfulfilled or neglected. For many of us these years offer unparalleled and unexpected openings into fresh capabilities, new insights, and uncommon adventures.

Entering Unknown Territory

Though I was not aware of what was happening at the beginning, the decade of my sixties turned out to be filled with major explorations, both outer and inner. I was on the threshold of a new, stimulating, and challenging stage of my life. Many newly discovered areas of study and creativity gave shape to my years of transition into old age.

After my children left home I looked for some activity that would satisfy my need for self-expression. I tried several things, one of which was renewing my interest in horses. After testing my skill at jumping, too many near-falls reminded me that I really was not at the right age to be indulging in that particular activity. I then turned to something physically safer and more artistic. After taking an introductory course at a local community college, I became a passionate fine art photographer. This creative outlet, which absorbed me for several years, led into an unforeseen domain, for my black-and-white still-life studies produced some curious, dark, and disturbing pictures that came unbidden from a hidden part of my psyche. Often I found myself sobbing as I watched the images emerge from their chemical baths in the darkroom. (This was before the time of digital photography.) I was driven to find out just what those distressing images meant.

Since I had been attending lectures and conferences on Jungian psychology, it seemed that one way to discover what my photographs revealed about my inner life was to work with a Jungian analyst. I was fortunate in finding a woman who grew up in the South as I had and who therefore understood the cultural milieu in which I spent my formative years. These sessions, though often painful, were immensely helpful in dealing with some of my concerns and conflicts, for we talked about my original family history, my marriage, and my mothering.

Most of all, though, we talked about my dreams. In a recurring dream I was at a university. The dreams persisted over a period of months, so one day my analyst suggested that perhaps I was being called to go back to school. Such a notion seemed preposterous—I was much too old. But when, just for a moment, I allowed myself to seriously consider such a possibility, my heart raced and my skin shivered with excitement. I realized that I had a deep desire for intellectual stimulation and psychological exploration and that indeed I was being called to return to school. So, at age sixty-nine I enrolled in a PhD program in Mythological Studies at Pacifica Graduate Institute in Southern California and completed my degree at age seventy-three.

As mentioned above, I began planning and participating in rituals for myself, my family, and friends. Some were personal and private, focusing on my inner struggles. Others involved life passages, such as the coming-of-age ceremonies I conducted for each of my grandchildren. There were also seasonal celebrations and ceremonies of release and renewal. Another type was a ritual that honored women (and men) of age. When I was sixty-five, two of my friends initiated me into the Sisterhood of Crones. Eighteen of us sat around a large table and talked about our mothers, grandmothers, and other women who had influenced our lives. By this time I was eager to embrace my aging, proud to be declared a

Crone, and wished to share my enthusiasm for this new stage of life with those close to me. I have since initiated a number of my women friends into their own years of Cronehood and have given men the honorary title of Elder.

Though I did not know it at the time, I have since learned that my unease and my search for meaning in my early sixties were not at all unusual. This period is pivotal for many of us, even if we do not at first recognize its onset or its significance. There comes a time, however, when we realize, as I did when I wrote that letter to my daughters, that we are growing old. Such an awareness can propel us into new ways of thinking and acting and being. It swings open a door into what was for me a profoundly enriching period of life.

My interest in aging led me to discover that many others have had similar experiences, and I have learned from their stories. One of my favorite examples of how encroaching age can bring on feelings of uncertainty is offered by Rabbi Zalman Schachter-Shalomi. As he tells it: "I was approaching my sixtieth birthday, and a feeling of futility had invaded my soul, plunging me into a state of depression that no amount of busyness or diversion could dispel.... At night, looking at myself in the mirror in unguarded moments, I realized that I was growing old." The rabbi decided to take a forty-day retreat during which he prayed, meditated, studied, and took long walks in order to sort out the reasons for his malaise. He began to see that he was shedding one phase of his life in preparation for his initiation as an elder, one who could use his (or her) experience and judgment and accrued wisdom for the benefit of society.

The rabbi thenceforth devoted his time and energies to helping others of this age group develop a process he called spiritual *eldering*, the purpose of which was to enable older people to awaken their spirituality, arouse their physical vitality, and become socially responsible "elders of the tribe." He wrote a book (along with Ronald S. Miller) about this titled *From Age-ing to Sage-ing*, a reminder that there can be an accumulation of insight and wisdom in our later years. He especially encouraged elders to serve as mentors for the young.

The poet May Sarton similarly became intensely aware of encroaching age as expressed in her long poem "Gestalt at Sixty," from which these lines are excerpted:

> I am not ready to die,
> But I am learning to trust death
> As I have trusted life.
> I am moving
> Toward a new freedom
> Born of detachment,
> And a sweeter grace—
> Learning to let go.
>
> I am not ready to die,
> But as I approach sixty
> I turn my face toward the sea.
> I shall go where tides replace time,
> Where my world will open to a far horizon.
>
> Over the floating, never-still flux and change.
> I shall go with the changes,
> I shall look far out over golden grasses
> And blue waters....
>
> There are no farewells.
> Praise God for his mercies,
> For His austere demands,
> For His light
> And for His darkness.

Sarton repeats the line "I am not ready to die" several times throughout the poem but goes on to say that as she approaches sixty she is "moving toward a new freedom/born of detachment,/And a sweeter grace—/ learning to let go." She sees changes coming, but vows to go with the changes.

In her book *No! I Don't Want to Join a Book Club: Dairy of a 60thYear*, Virginia Ironside addresses the age of sixty with a hilarious depiction of how one woman (perhaps herself) lets go of middle age and moves on in life. As her character Marie puts it, "Now, nearly sixty, I feel like a young and lissome old person. I feel like a new and shiny snake that has shed a middle-aged skin that was getting horribly worn, smelly and tatty." Her witty comments and refreshing outlook give us an inspiring and revitalizing view on how to embrace the aging process. She also has captured the sense of what it is like to be one of the "young old."

Whereas for many of us reaching this age offers new opportunities for learning and exploration, Marie argues that being sixty liberates her from expectations she placed on herself earlier in her life. She no longer feels guilty, for example, about not learning another language, for she feels it is no longer a useful goal. "I find, approaching sixty," she says, "that the great pleasure is that so many things are *impossible*." Not only that, she says, "my past will be truly bigger than my future. And I like it like that." She proudly claims that she has "done young" and wants to start doing *old* things. Her attitude is that of one who has been freed from the heavy responsibilities of earlier years.

Attending to the Heart

In a more serious vein, Jane Prétat, a Jungian analyst and family therapist, considers this period transitional, a passageway between one way of being and another. She sees it as a time of preparation for the final stage of our lives and suggests that we would do well to pay attention to what is going on in our bodies, in our minds, and in our hearts, so that we might use these years wisely. She points out that our bodies, with their increasing aches and pains, demand that we slow down. Once slowed, we can then pay attention to our breathing, become more meditative, and quiet our inner noise. Through such quietude we can develop a great wonder about how our bodies work and what we may learn from them; we can tune in to our thoughts and feelings and thus become better acquainted with our selves. It is her belief that by developing our awareness, we can learn to live more fully and also face our impending deaths with greater acceptance and less fear.

Another perspective on sixty is offered by a woman who had dreamed for years of walking the ancient pilgrimage trail, El Camino de Santiago de Compostela, but who had not taken any of the necessary practical steps to make it happen. She was struck one cold January morning with the thought "If I do not walk the Camino during this, my sixtieth year, I will never go, and MY LIFE WILL BE FORFEIT!" This message, which she says came from *outside* herself, made it clear that if she did not do this, she would have failed to fulfill her life's purpose. She felt called to make the journey because it offered her opportunities for spiritual growth. After receiving this directive, she began in earnest to raise funds, make arrangements for her family during her absence, gather the gear she would need, and get her physical body in shape. She fought her fears, faced her vulnerabilities and, seemingly miraculously, everything fell into place, and she made her trek.

In her account of the experience, she wrote:

> Spain, my Camino, my sixtieth birthday on the
> Camino, all were more than I could ever have
> imagined, time out of ordinary time, producing a shift
> in me. I did learn to trust: to trust in the kindness of
> friends and strangers, to trust in myself, and to trust
> that there is a Higher Power guiding my path.... Trust
> has not become second nature to me, but a close friend
> I can call on at any time by choosing to remember all
> the gifts of my Camino.

Learning to trust in others and in oneself is a major accomplishment at any age.

In the Hindu tradition, the age of sixty has long been acknowledged as of great significance and is the occasion for a special celebration called *shastipurti*. Sixty in that culture represents a transition from the life-stage of householder, a person focused on the needs of family or profession, to that of forest dweller, one who begins to separate from the daily demands of life in order to spend more time in contemplation and in preparation for death. Though we in the West do not call ourselves forest dwellers, some of us who have passed sixty instinctively follow a similar pattern in that we begin to spend less time focused on outer accomplishments and more on inner goals. We may not acknowledge our transition with the kind of ritual celebration that is common among many Hindus, but at some level we know that we have crossed over into a new stage of our lives.

The American spiritual teacher Ram Dass, author of *Still Here: Embracing Aging, Changing, and Dying*, happened to be in India on his sixtieth birthday and was accorded the appropriate celebration by his Hindu hosts. Since he had dedicated his life to a spiritual path, he tried to focus on finishing up his worldly affairs and forgoing worldly pleasures. It took two years before he began to admit his senior citizen status, an identity that at first made him troubled and anxious. He came to understand, however, that we cannot win if we choose to fight against natural law, calling such a battle "inhumane, toward both ourselves and the cycle of life."

Once Ram Dass embraced his own later stage of life, he began devoting himself to giving seminars and retreats focused on the issues surrounding aging, dying, and death. But it was not until he suffered a serious stroke at age sixty-five that he was given an unwelcome test of some of his own pronouncements and recommendations. Suddenly he was no longer the helper but the one being helped, for he was left partially paralyzed and suffered from severe speech impairment. Nevertheless, after many hours of rehabilitation and still in a wheelchair, he resumed his lecture schedule, speaking slowly, which, he says, means that silence "arises without my control and allows for a sense of emptiness, an emptiness that listeners can use as a doorway to their inner quiet." Ram Dass's willingness to share his personal disabilities in a public arena serves as an inspiring example as we begin to face our own aging.

Following a Personal Path

Cathleen Rountree interviewed women in their sixties and published their stories in one of a series of books she has written about women at different stages of life. She found in these women "an increased level of self-confidence and personal authority, a deepening trust of the inner process, and an ability to be present in, pay attention to, and appreciate the 'now.'" She describes her interviewees as "gutsy, dauntless, and emboldened to be exactly who they are and to say exactly what they think and feel." As Rountree observed, sixty and the years beyond can be a time of discovery, particularly in terms of establishing one's personal authenticity.

As it was for me and for many others, the decade of our sixties can be a gateway to a new way of life, an opportunity to expand our horizons, to try out something unfamiliar and untried, something challenging and arduous. It might mean taking on the responsibilities of a mentor or consciously assuming the role of elder for our friends and family. We might spend time reflecting on what we have learned from our successes and failures. On the other hand, sixty might represent, as for semi-fictional Marie, a sense of joyful liberation, offering release from formerly stultifying expectations and unrealistic goals. It might be a chance to retire from family or business responsibilities, becoming a "forest dweller," making room for more leisure, more relaxation, more time for introspection and contemplation. It might be an occasion to follow some of Robert Johnson's suggestions (outlined in his book *Living Your Unlived*

Life: Coping with Unrealized Dreams and Fulfilling Your Purpose in the Second Half of Life), such as unlocking hidden talents, seizing "dangerous" opportunities, mastering the art of being truly alive in the present moment, and revitalizing a connection with symbolic life. As Gay Gaer Luce observes, "A person of sixty can grow as much as a child of six. The later years are a time for self-development, emancipation, a spiritual growth." The truth of these words continues to validate my own experience and that of many others whom I know.

Sixty may generate a desire to discover the purpose and meaning of the path we have followed. We may search for greater understanding and acceptance of the decisions we have made. We may seek for a more meaningful connection to our religious heritage or look for new ways of expressing our spiritual yearnings. We may wish to right old wrongs or express gratitude for gifts received. We may experience an unexpected feeling of liberation as we are finally free of wearying responsibilities and oppressive demands.

John Cowper Powys, who died in 1963 at age ninety-one, observed that much can be learned by observing other old things, such as animals and even trees. He wisely admonishes us: "But if by the time we're sixty we haven't learnt what a knot of paradox and contradiction life is, and how exquisitely the good and the bad are mingled in every action we take, and what a compromising hostess Our Lady of Truth is, we haven't grown old to much purpose." We would all do well to attend to his words.

However we live into this decade of our lives, the awareness of being sixty years old can bring renewed energy, increased creativity, and a delightful discovery of formerly unrecognized talents and interests. Whatever path we choose, this decade may well mark the beginning of our adventurous journey into old age. It is up to us to decide how best to spend these precious remaining years.

∼

Dass, Ram. *Still Here: Embracing Aging, Changing, and Dying.* Eds. Mark Matousek and Marlene Roeder. New York: Penguin, 2000.

Glasgow, Ellen. *The Woman Within.* New York: Harcourt Brace Jovanovich, 1954.

Ironside, Virginia. *No! I Don't Want to Join a Book Club: Diary of a 60th Year.* New York: Viking, 2006.

Johnson, Robert A. and Jerry M. Ruhl. *Living Your Unlived Life: Coping with Unrealized Dreams and Fulfilling Your Purpose in the Second Half of Life.* New York: Tarcher/Penguin, 2007.

Luce, Gay Gaer. *Your Second Life: Vitality and Growth in Middle and Later Years.* New York: Delacorte Press, 1979.

Powys, John Cowper. *The Art of Growing Old.* New York: Village Press, 1944.

Prétat, Jane R. *Coming to Age: The Croning Years and Late-Life Transformation.* Toronto: Inner City Books, 1994.

Rountree, Cathleen. *On Women Turning 60: Embracing the Age of Fulfillment.* New York: Harmony Books, 1997.

Sarton, May. *End Game: A Journal of the Seventy-Ninth Year.* New York: Norton, 1992.

Schachter-Shalomi, Zalman, and Ronald S. Miller. *From Age-ing to Sage-ing: A Profound New Vision of Growing Older.* New York: Warner, 1995.

Weltman, Deborah Terra. "Gifts of the Camino," in *Healing Through the Numinous from a Jungian Perspective.* Ed. Christy Beckmann. St. Louis: C. G. Jung Society of St. Louis, 2013.

The Language of Aging

*For we all of us, grave or light, get our thoughts entangled
in metaphors, and act fatally on the strength of them.*

George Eliot
Middlemarch

The Power of Words

The words we use shape the world we inhabit. As an example, in the first
chapter I pointed out how the descriptive word "old" has become
contaminated by unpleasant associations, making its usage laden with
suggestions of negativity regarding aging. I have also noticed that for
some strange reason many of the terms commonly associated with aging
begin with "d" and have detrimental, even frightening, connotations:
*disease, decline, decay, descent, depression, deficiency, debility, despair,
dependency, disability, decrepitude, diminishment, deterioration*, and, not
to be ignored, those most dreaded d-words, *demise* and *death*.

These terms certainly hold some truth, since our bodies do decline in
strength, we are from time to time depressed about our debilities, we do
get diseases, our slower gait indicates a measure of decrepitude, our
hearing and eyesight may have deteriorated, and we shall not escape our
eventual demise. But might there be other terms less discouraging, more
reassuring, and more representative of the many alternative realities in
our various stages of old age?

For a moment just imagine how our outlook might change if we broadened our everyday thinking and usage concerning aging by moving down the alphabet by one letter to include expressions like these beginning with the letter "e": the *experience* gained through a long lifetime, the *expansion* that takes place within us as we amass more information, the *extensiveness* of the history we embody, the personal *enrichment* that grows out of our relationships, the steady *evolution* of our character, our continued *engagement* with the world, the *enlargement* of our understanding and acceptance, as well as the *enhancement*, possibly even *enlightenment*, due to our maturing emotional and spiritual insights. There is even the possibility of becoming more *erudite* as we age, and if we are really lucky, we can even reach that highly desirable state of *equilibrium*.

As another example, we have become accustomed to think of aging as *loss*. After all, once past middle age we are likely to start losing our youthful vitality, our physical flexibility and strength, our short-term memory, our unblemished skin and abundant hair, and often our power and influence. We also begin to lose old friends. Though these losses cannot and should not be denied, what if instead of always thinking of aging only as loss, we recognize that aging can also be characterized by *gain*? If you think about it, there is much that is or can be added to our existence as we age: accumulated knowledge, augmented experience, more complex neural patterns, greater patience, deeper insights, increased awareness, better understanding, heightened acceptance, a sense of serenity, and perhaps even a measure of wisdom.

And what if instead of focusing on our *deficiencies*, we thought in terms of our *proficiencies*, all the skills, knowledge, and expertise we have gathered during our years? That would help us direct our attention toward what we have to offer, ways we can use our abilities in service to our communities. There are many organizations that would benefit from our lifetime of knowledge and experience, and there are opportunities to give back to our neighborhoods, such as participating in local food or clothing drives. We can volunteer in schools or share our talents in churches, synagogues, mosques, or community centers. Our involvement can not only be of help to the younger generation and those less advantaged, it also can benefit us by keeping us engaged and active. Furthermore, by stressing our sufficiencies rather than grumbling about our insufficiencies we can change the way we think of ourselves.

The point is that by choosing different words and phrases we might change our concepts and outlook and instead of viewing aging through the lens of loss and privation, we can look to its promise of gain and abundance. If we develop this kind of linguistic sensibility, our conversations will reinforce our confidence in ourselves and inspire young people who know us to look to us as worthy role models. We can begin to celebrate the long fruitful history we embody and cherish the longevity with which we have been blessed. We can be assured that we can be old without being diminished.

Symbolic Language

There are many other examples demonstrating that the way we think and what we do is profoundly affected by our language, not only by single words, but also by the metaphors we routinely employ. Metaphorical constructions are sometimes considered a specialized kind of discourse characteristic of poetic imagination, but, as expressed through ordinary speech and behavior, they are pervasive and extremely influential in our lives. George Lakoff and Mark Johnson in their book *Metaphors We Live By* contend that the way we think and act is in fact fundamentally metaphorical. This notion that our conceptual systems consist largely of metaphor has made me more sensitive to the kind of speech I use and hear, especially when there is talk about aging and old age. Since our thoughts do indeed get "entangled in metaphors," as George Eliot observed, we should heed which ones we use.

Symbols, metaphors, and archetypal images bridge that space between our outer and inner realities, suggesting that our lives unfold somewhere between our outer consciousness and the depths of our unconscious. As the psychologist Robert Romanyshyn explains,

> A symbol holds the tension between what is visible and what is invisible, between, we might say, what shows itself in the light and what hides itself in darkness, and as such it requires for its expression a language that hints at meaning and does not attempt to define it or pin it down. Metaphor is such a language….

He suggests that one reason we are drawn to metaphor is that it evokes an image as opposed to an empirical fact or rational idea. In other words, metaphor triggers the imagination, thus enriching our perspective. So perhaps it is our imagination that needs to be expanded and strengthened regarding the way we think of aging.

Jung used the word *archetypes* to describe what he believed to be universal patterns which tend to produce similar ideas and behavior even in widely differing individuals. Common examples might be mother, father, or friend. These pre-existent forms constitute what has come to be known as the collective unconscious, a kind of universal sea of potential images and behaviors from which humankind draws its diverse nature.

My study of mythology and depth psychology in my seventies helped me become aware of the ancient Greek deities as examples of archetypes. Because of my age I at first identified strongly with Hekate, the old crone. She was powerful, complex, and frequently maligned, as are some old women today. The dictionary says that a crone is "a withered old woman," but I would say that we are not *withered*, but *weathered*, since old women like me have been exposed to a lot of life's turbulence, thus becoming tough and resilient. We have developed our own appealing patina and complexity after facing and overcoming a lifetime of complicated issues.

As mentioned in the Introduction, I have been reflecting on my identity. Though I have many qualities in common with Hekate, the archetype that has most profoundly influenced my life is Hestia, goddess of the hearth. Actually, she is the fire itself, or more precisely, the embers that were kept alive in the center of every ancient Greek home. That fire represented the integrity of the home. Disputes were settled there, oaths sworn there, and embers from the mother's home were taken to that of her newly married daughters in order to establish family continuity. Hestia was not only the literal center of the round Greek houses, she also was the centering, grounding force that held the family and the household together. Seeing myself as an embodiment of the Hestia archetype has helped me understand many of the choices I have made in my life.

In our later years, when we find ourselves ever more confused and confounded by a rapidly changing world and distressed by incomprehensible current events, the image of Hestia helps us more deeply appreciate and explore our *center*, the stable and secure place we return to over and over again and yet discover anew each time, a place T. S. Eliot describes as being "at the still point of the turning world." We would do well to emulate Hestia's sedentary, quiescent, and imperturbable manner as we become less mobile. She can be our guide as we learn to sit quietly in contemplation and meditation in order to develop greater insight into our soul's workings.

The language of metaphor and the concept of archetypes help us understand something about our mysterious deeper selves, those parts that we cannot directly or fully access but glimpse through dreams and fantasies. We are often unable to find words that adequately express our most profound feelings and therefore must rely, as Romanyshyn says, on "a way of speaking in the gap between meaning and the absence of meaning, a way of speaking of meaning as a presence that is haunted by absence." Metaphor is used to express the inexpressible by hinting at hidden meanings through drawing unexpected and intriguing parallels.

The French philosopher Gaston Bachelard says that "a metaphor gives concrete substance to an impression that is difficult to express." He notes that in attempting to acquire a more imaginative use of language we must seek "in every word" the desire for "double meaning, for metaphor." Such usage is often ambiguous, alluding to and drawing us into a larger mystery. It opens our minds to the imaginal, to new possibilities, to new ways of seeing. Writers of all kinds have engaged our interest by employing a variety of fascinating images for the realities of encroaching age.

It is important that we keep these concepts in mind as we think about how to describe our life span, especially when we talk about growing old, for the symbols and the metaphors we apply reveal something of our often semi-concealed attitudes and beliefs. Again, it is not that we should deny the inevitable nature of aging; we need not reject the negative to embrace the positive. But by developing a metaphoric sensibility such that our language reinforces more realistic and affirming aspects of this stage of our lives, we will more accurately describe our totality, increase our self-confidence, and allow us to more fully appreciate the gifts of aging.

The Seasons of Life

One of the most common metaphors describing both the totality of our life span and that of old age is that of the seasons. I am reminded of a time in my early sixties when I spent a week alone in the country. One day, as I sat looking onto a forest of towering trees outside the windows of my sylvan sanctuary, suddenly a storm arose. The wind blew in mighty gusts, and torrential rains spilled from the heavy clouds. The downpour was quickly absorbed into the soil, feeding the thirsty roots of the trees. As I watched in awe and wonderment at the power and beauty of it all, I thought of the sweet life-giving rain, water that would help sustain the trees through the coming autumn and winter. And I was struck with the sobering thought that I was facing those same seasons, the autumn and winter of my own life.

Though autumn is the time when the greenness and vitality of summer are fading, when the leaves turn brown, shrivel, and fall to the ground, it also is a time of unparalleled beauty. Before those leaves actually let go, they give us a great gift of riotous color, bursting forth in a final display of enthusiasm and exultation. There are also flowers that withhold their blooming until the weather has cooled and much of the garden has finished its show of color. In the months of autumn we have the magnificent chrysanthemum, Japanese symbol of that which is enduring, luxurious, and whole, the "one who shows her beauty late."

Just as the word *late* refers to a delayed flowering or ripening, such as a second batch of strawberries appearing towards the end of the season, the term *late life* can remind us that we also have the ability to bloom or exhibit an unexpected bonus of growth, even though we are, in some respects, past our prime. Many examples of late bloomers can be cited, such as Grandma Moses, who started a successful career as a folk artist in her nineties. Sophocles wrote "Oedipus at Colonus" at age ninety-two. Though not so illustrious, I count myself among these, for I enrolled in graduate school at age sixty-nine and received a PhD at age seventy-three.

Just as I watched the rain nourishing that forest in the fall, we may in our autumn years retain a reservoir of sweet knowledge deep within that contributes to our ability to continue to grow intellectually and spiritually, that enables us—if we pay attention and work at it—to mature into old persons who are still learning, still pursuing joy, and whose lives still hold promise for the future. That kind of deeper knowledge is what leads to wisdom. It is up to us to find that reserve and draw upon it to sustain our inner growth, while letting go of attitudes that no longer contribute to our well-being. Just as the trees in autumn shed their leaves in preparation for the dormancy of winter, so in this stage of life we can begin to discard desiccated, depleted, and damaging beliefs regarding what it means to grow old.

The Days of Our Lives

The daily passage of the sun as the imagined trajectory of our lives is a metaphor postulated by C. G. Jung. Thus morning represents our young years, a time of biological growth with focus on building family and career. High noon, the zenith, is midlife, the culmination point, but also a time of transition from an emphasis on outward matters to more inward concerns. In Jung's view, afternoon, with its slow withdrawal of light, initiates a time for reflection on the meaning of life, a deeper consciousness, and a search for spiritual understanding. A reference to the "afternoon of life," meaning a time past middle age, reminds us that the ending of the day is marked by sunset, which Bachelard describes as a "decline marked with fire, a last protest, a call to beauty"— similar to the late-season chrysanthemum's radiant bloom.

Another image for that later period of the day, and of our lives, is twilight, after the sun goes down but before darkness descends. Twilight comes from the Old English *twi*, meaning "two," which suggests a doubling, perhaps a combination of light and dark. But a more appropriate sense might be that of "half-light," an in-between time, a transition between light and not-light. It is a time for us to linger in the early evening before the emerging darkness overcomes the waning light, just as we might spend our twilight years in thoughtful reflection. The idea of a diminution of light can suggest loss and sadness, a sense of brooding, a waiting to be summoned, but as we all know, twilight following the often glorious colors of sunset is often a beautiful, soft, and gentle time of day. So it can be with this time of our lives.

Old Age as Ripening

Another interesting metaphor suggests that our later years can be likened to that time when the fruit has completed its growth but continues to ripen. The aging philosopher Cicero pointed out that "just as apples when they are green are with difficulty plucked from the tree, but when ripe and mellow fall of themselves, so, with the young, death comes as a result of force, while with the old it is the result of ripeness." He goes on to say that "the thought of this 'ripeness' for death is so pleasant, that the nearer I approach death the more I feel like one who is in sight of land at last and is about to anchor in his home port after a long voyage."

The contemporary American writer and food critic Jeffrey Steingarten enhances our sense of the image when he describes ripening as "a tightly structured, programmed series of changes a fruit undergoes as it prepares to seduce every gastronomically aware animal in the neighborhood." He sees these changes as making the fruit more appealing just when the seeds are preparing to germinate. Another writer, Stewart Edward White, observes, "The thing you are ripening toward is the fruit of your life. It will make you bright inside, no matter what you are outside. It is a shining thing."

In this poem D. H. Lawrence, in 1929, also compared late life to a ripened fruit:

> When the ripe fruit falls
> its sweetness distils and trickles away into the
> veins of the earth.
>
> When fulfilled people die
> the essential oil of their experience enters
> the veins of living space, and adds a glisten
> to the atom, to the body of immortal chaos.
>
> For space is alive
> and it stirs like a swan
> whose feathers glisten
> silky with oil of distilled experience.

Perhaps if we thought of the aging process as filling ourselves with tinctures of oil, alluring and seductive, we would more fully appreciate all that we have to offer as we grow old. The later stages of our lives are, in fact, our time of ripening, of slowly reaching the peak of our fruitful essence. Such a thought may seem outrageous to those who hold a pessimistic view of aging, but certainly it is more pleasant to think of ourselves as ripening than rotting. I like to imagine this late age metaphorically as a velvety, luscious, ripened peach—delicate and soft, brimming with the sweet juiciness of our lives, preparing but not quite ready to fall from the tree.

Life as Journey

A common metaphor for our passage through life is that of a journey; from birth onward we are in constant motion, advancing from one growth cycle to the next. As we near the end of our lives it is as if we are nearing the end of our travels. Before then we are wanderers, meandering our way through the years, occasionally walking straight ahead on a clear path, but more often taking shortcuts or following detours, climbing mountains and descending into valleys, getting lost, finding the way, and if all goes well—or if it does not—reaching our final destination. All too often we are not aware that we have passed a significant age marker along the way. We walked right past without even noticing or pausing to consider its significance. At some juncture, however, a jarring misstep or unexpected barrier may stop us in our tracks. We may find ourselves confused, adrift, uncertain just where we are, as Dante describes in his famous lines in *The Divine Comedy:*

> In the middle of the journey of our life
> I found myself astray in a dark wood
> Where the straight road had been lost sight of.

As Dante suggests, our paths can veer off the straightway, or the road ahead appear shrouded in fog, and we find ourselves lost, uncertain which way to turn. The search for the trail may be intriguing as we ponder which road is the right one—if there is, indeed, a "right" one.

Some of the byways and seeming dead-ends may, in fact, be more scenic, more interesting, and as "right" as the main road. There are adventures to be had and discoveries to be made in all those places of uncertainty as we make our way along the highways and low ways of life.

In Robert Frost's "The Road Not Taken," the traveler must choose one of two paths. The final two stanzas suggest that whatever choice is made will result in lasting consequences.

> And both that morning equally lay
> In leaves no step had trodden black.
> Oh, I kept the first for another day!
> Yet knowing how way leads on to way,
> I doubted if I should ever come back.
>
> I shall be telling this with a sigh
> Somewhere ages and ages hence:
> Two roads diverged in a wood, and I—
> I took the one less traveled by,
> And that has made all the difference.

These poems and observations, and others like them, address the course of our lives by speaking to our imagination, and thus enlarge and enrich our perceptions of the choices we have made and continue to make. I have often wondered what my life would have been like had I not decided at age eighteen to run away from my home in North Carolina to find a new life in the Midwest. Surely that decision, as Frost writes, "has made all the difference." Just as "the one less traveled by" suggests unexpected possibility, poetic images frequently provide us with hope, reassurance, and solace. Though we may go off the beaten track, or not see our path clearly, or make different kinds of choices, there is still comfort in knowing that others—poets, speaking for all of us—have pondered these dilemmas. In sharing with us their own struggles with darkness and uncertainty, what it is like to not clearly see the road ahead, they illuminate the human journey.

Life as River

Comparison to a river is yet another symbolic way to view our lifespan. I live in St. Louis, a city on the Mississippi River, and I often think of its path down the center of our country as a metaphor for my life. Just as the Mississippi, drawing from rivulets, streams, and larger tributaries in its course through the heartland of America, flows determinedly, if tortuously, from its origins in the north to its inevitable dissolution in the south, so our lives travel in one irreversible though meandering direction from birth to death. We are also a mixture of many confluences, major and minor, arising from our biological origins and contributed to by our life experiences.

My life, like many others, and like the river, has had periods of turbulence and of calm. Sometimes I am flooded with over-activity, my life churning with too many demands and too much commotion. Other times I am slowed down by lethargy and boredom, sluggish from lack of stimulation or motivation. And then there are the occasions of blessed tranquility when the river of my life flows easily and smoothly.

Points of confluence can be challenging, when our placid flow is disturbed by a surge of new experience—marriage, the birth of a child or a grandchild, a new job, moving to a new place. At times such streams entering the river of our lives introduce contamination, comparable to psychologically dangerous toxins—personal or business failure, severe illness, ruptured friendship, a period of hopelessness. In the river of my life, there have been persons and events that brought enormous pleasure and vitality while others have brought impurity, draining me of energy, leaving me tired and irritable.

The image of a river also brings to mind the vessels that float on its surface. Many times in this life journey I have been carried along like a boat on the current of daily life, with no notion of direction or destination. At times I erred in my navigational judgment and capsized, nearly drowning in the dark undertow of my unconscious. Early in my adult life there were instances when I could not speak for hours, rendered literally dumbstruck by inner conflict. Other times I have run aground, gotten stuck in the dark deep mud of depression, unable to extricate myself from despair. In a sense we are both the boat negotiating strong or slow-moving currents and the river with its wholesome and troublesome tributaries. We pass through sublime vistas and encounter threatening landscapes. In living our daily lives with some conscious awareness, we re-unify, re-member, re-vision, gather together the multiple streams and strands that have, by some awesome and mysterious process, been poured into the riverbed that contains and directs our vital energies into one lifetime. The notion of a river and its boat can carry us a long way, and all of us, to some extent, live this metaphor. Bertrand Russell observed:

> An individual's human existence should be like a river—small at first, narrowly contained within its bounds, and seeking passionately past boulders and even waterfalls. Gradually the river grows wide, the banks recede, the waters flow more quietly and in the end without any visible break they become merged in the sea and painlessly lose their individual being.

Before the river empties into the sea, it spreads out into the delta, which metaphorically is comparable to the last stage of our lives. The soil of the delta, at least historically, is incredibly rich, for deposited there is an accumulation of minerals from the various regions that have found their way through tributaries into the waters of the majestic river. Just as the river has offered its gift of richness to the delta before it is consumed by the vastness of the sea, so in our old age we have the opportunity to share our accumulated knowledge, experience, and wisdom with those we know and love before we enter the great beyond.

———

It matters not whether we imagine ourselves in the autumn of our lives, perhaps nearing the quiet of winter; or delighting in the twilight of our years as we await the night; or envisioning ourselves as deliciously ripened fruit, ready for the picking; or fancy ourselves close to the end of our long, circuitous journey; or floating down the river of life on the verge of emptying into the sea. Regardless of the metaphor we choose, there is no question but that the language we use has tremendous influence on how we view ourselves and others as we grow old. I personally like the image of the river spreading its gifts at the delta before being absorbed into the sea, a symbol of that mysterious realm which lies beyond our knowing.

～

Bachelard, Gaston. *On Poetic Imagination and Reverie.* Trans. Colette Gaudin. Dallas: Spring Publications, 1971.

Cicero, Marcus Tullius. *De Senectute,* vol. 20. *Cicero's Works.* Trans. William A. Falconer. Cambridge, MA: Harvard University Press, 1971.

Dante Alighieri. *Dante's Inferno: Translations by Twenty Contemporary Poets.* Ed. Daniel Halpern. New York: Ecco Press, 1993.

Eliot, George. *Middlemarch.* Rev. ed. New York: Penguin, 2003.

Eliot, T. S. "Four Quartets," *Collected Poems 1909-1962.* New York: Harcourt Brace Jovanovich, 1991.

Frost, Robert. *Complete Poems of Robert Frost.* New York: Henry Holt, 1949.

Jung, C. G. "The Stages of Life," in *The Collected Works of C. G. Jung,* vol. 8. Ed. and trans. Gerhard Adler and R. F. C. Hull. Princeton, NJ: Princeton University Press, 1960.

Lakoff, George, and Mark Johnson. *Metaphors We Live By.* Chicago: University of Chicago Press, 1980.

Lawrence, D. H. *The Complete Poems of D. H. Lawrence*. New York: Penguin, 1994.

Romanyshyn, Robert D. The Wounded *Researcher: Research with Soul in Mind*. New Orleans: Spring Journal Books, 2007.

Russell, Bertrand. *Portraits from Memory and Other Essays*. New York: Simon & Schuster, 1950.

Steingarten, Jeffrey. "Ripe Now." *Vogue*. July 1992.

White, Stewart Edward. *With Folded Wings*. New York: Dutton, 1947.

Seventy—Settling into Ourselves

A human being would certainly not grow to be seventy or eighty years old if this longevity had no meaning for the species. The afternoon of human life must also have a significance of its own and cannot be merely a pitiful appendage to life's morning.

C. G. Jung
"On the Psychology of the Unconscious"

The Middle Stage of Aging

In my seventies and early eighties I began to come to terms in a more substantial way with where I was in life; I arrived at an indisputable realization that I was transitioning into true old age. I had moved from young old to middle old. As I thought about this period it occurred to me that in certain respects it is reminiscent of adolescence. There are similar highs and lows, delightful times and miserable times, all contributing to sporadic feelings of confusion and uncertainty. In our teen years we are neither child nor adult, but somewhere in between. In our middle stage of aging we are again in between, neither among the youngest of the old nor yet one of the oldest. Like our adolescent selves, our bodies are going through profound physical and hormonal changes. Our emotions may be volatile as we are called upon to make difficult life adjustments. As teenagers we were striving to establish our independence, but we may now find ourselves becoming more dependent. As we grew out of our teen years most of us left our childhood homes, and now we may again be forced to move from our familiar surroundings. We find ourselves once more in a passage from one way of life to another.

As mentioned in the chapter on being sixty, I enrolled in graduate school at age sixty-nine, a surprising undertaking at that time of life. For three years I flew once a month from my Midwestern city to Southern California for a few days of intensive lectures, followed by weeks of serious reading, study, and writing papers at home. After that were two years researching and writing a dissertation. Not everyone would find such an activity at this stage of life possible or even desirable, but I was a "late bloomer," thrilled to discover within myself previously unrecognized capabilities and unappreciated potentials.

Relating to classmates of varied ages and backgrounds, attending lectures, writing papers, and immersing myself in the research required for a dissertation presented significant challenges. I had not been in an academic environment for forty-five years, so needless to say it took considerable courage to take on such a taxing travel and study schedule. But going back to school at my age was without question one of the most important and gratifying accomplishments of my life, done solely for personal enrichment and fulfillment. I felt liberated from my former identity as only wife and mother, becoming instead, or in addition to, a student among students, noticeably older than my classmates, but pleased to discover a whole new way of being in the world—an explorer extraordinaire. Those years were an exhilarating, intoxicating, life-changing experience. For me, this stage of life did appear, as Jung says, to have a meaning all its own.

New Adventures

Though mine was perhaps an unusual path, many persons in this middle stage of old age still have the desire for new and meaningful activities. They accept the reality of their chronological age and the accompanying limitations while retaining their vitality, curiosity, and willingness to embark on new adventures, determined to make good use of the years they have left. For example, those not wishing the structure or demands of an academic degree, but still desirous of additional learning, can take advantage of organizations such as Lifelong Learning Institutes, Road Scholar, and community centers that provide classes for continued intellectual stimulation and artistic expression. More and more older persons are participating in such programs.

We have learned that it is important to keep our brains engaged, and there are many ways of doing that aside from academic pursuits. Some of us find opportunities for volunteer work, a way of giving back to the community, whether in schools, religious groups, or homeless shelters. We may play games (a friend of mine in her eighties is now learning to play bridge), and puzzles challenge our ability to see patterns and organize our visual perception. Golf is a good way to get exercise and enhance a skill. Taking music or art classes can stimulate our minds and at the same time develop physical coordination and flexibility. In addition to walking and other sensible exercise, for example, activities like gentle yoga and t'ai chi ch'uan can be helpful maintaining physical and mental fitness.

Once we grasp the notion that we probably have a decade or more for new endeavors and further explorations, we are willing—sometimes compelled—to fulfill formerly unacknowledged or unachieved dreams or ambitions. Whatever our interests or preferences, many of us are finally able to do those things we did not have opportunities or time for earlier in our lives, especially if we have the advantages of economic security and relatively good health. I have a number of friends in their seventies who have found new enthusiasms: one has become a master gardener, another is pursuing a path of Buddhist meditation; still another has written a play which was produced locally. Though (again like adolescents) we are likely to have some major upheavals and disruptions during this period of life, we are likely to have more free time than ever before, so are able to investigate fresh ideas and engage in new pursuits.

The crucial point is to find what gives pleasure and satisfaction, what arouses our passion and deepens our sense of self. However we go about it, and whatever our intellectual interests, craving for creativity, or level of physical vigor, this can be an exceedingly rich and creative time of life. Entering the middle phase of old age brings the penetrating knowledge that our time of being young is truly and forever past, that we are firmly fixed in our later years and must come to terms with the fact that we are now members of the older generation. But that does not mean giving up the desire for further learning. In fact, this stage of life often seems to inspire forays into previously unexplored interests.

Lessons Learned

Since many of us will remain free of major illness during our seventies, the full realization of this new stage of life may seep into our conscious awareness slowly, our attention increasingly focused on non-life-threatening physical disabilities such as stiff knees, reduced energy, or fading eyesight and hearing. Others of us will have to deal with a sudden serious infirmity that requires substantial adjustments in how we live. In addition to the opportunities for expanded learning and for growth, we are likely during this decade to face losses and disruptions to our lives, perhaps the illness or death of a mate or of a close friend. These experiences also offer us valuable lessons regarding how best to deal with the realities of this stage of life.

In my case the thrill of being in a PhD program was disrupted by deeply distressing news when my husband was diagnosed with Alzheimer's disease. It seemed ironic that as I was ascending the ladder of academic accomplishment, my brilliant husband, who after a successful career in business had in his retirement years written two books on the philosophy of physics, was descending into dementia. In the early years he remained reasonably functional, so that I could finish my studies without undue worry about his well-being. But as the disease progressed, he became more and more dependent, and by the time my studies were complete, I moved into the role of full-time caregiver.

In addition, shortly after my graduation, our daughter, in her late forties, was diagnosed with a rare, aggressive, life-threatening cancer. So while being caregiver for my husband I was at the same time supporting and helping her through surgeries, chemotherapy, and radiation treatments, the effects of which on several occasions brought her perilously close to death. Having to face the possibility of losing a daughter and already slowly losing a husband brought me to a new level of understanding of the perils and trials of old age. Those terrible, despairing experiences brought days of grief and deep depression, but they also taught me important lessons about life and about myself.

One lesson I learned was patience. Some persons with dementia become aggressive and unpleasant, but fortunately that was not the case with my husband, who remained sweet and gentle. But in the early stages of the disease he was endlessly repetitive; there was one period when he told me hundreds of times each day how important it is to have compassion, advice which, due to its tiresome recurrence, greatly tested my capacity to follow his worthy instruction. He also saw no reason to hurry, often taking hours to get dressed, no matter how urgent the circumstances. I discovered that it made life easier if I adjusted to his sense of time, avoiding the wasteful expenditure of energy required by demanding punctuality of someone incapable of being hurried.

Another lesson learned was acceptance. When our daughter was so extremely ill, I was frequently advised to emphasize the positive, to focus on her recovery, to think only bright thoughts, but I could see that this approach was not helpful to her or to me. I knew that I was not in control of the situation, so I eventually came to believe and accept that whatever path she took, whatever her soul chose to do, would be all right. This radical acceptance actually brought me peace and comfort. I was learning to truly appreciate the cycles and seasons that give life its beauty and its mystery. Of course I do not deny my joyful relief when she chose life.

The same level of acceptance was important in dealing with my husband's illness. He often seemed to live in another world, talking of travels to foreign countries, having conversations with imaginary persons, often confusing me for his mother. I made no effort to correct these misperceptions but rather showed interest in his nightly excursions, was curious about his conversations, and felt honored to be confused with his mother, a woman he loved deeply. Of course I also cried copious tears during those years of his decline, mourning the slow loss of the man to whom I had been married for almost sixty years.

A sense of detachment is another aspect of life that does not seem readily available when we are young but is helpful in our later years. Being detached does not mean that we no longer care, but it does mean that we do not feel quite so invested in specific outcomes. There is the ability to stand back, as if viewing things from a distance, showing interest but not feeling a need to direct. I find that particularly true in my relationship with my grandchildren and great-grandchildren. I am delighted with their growth and fascinated as I watch their personalities emerge, but though I am willing to offer help or advice if asked, I feel no desire to shape their lives according to my own standards. I have a measure of detachment.

An additional feature of detachment is that we come to recognize that life is not made up of blacks and whites, wrongs and rights, but large areas of gray, replete with mixtures of both right and wrong. It's as if we have enough distance to see and appreciate a broader horizon, an expanded spectrum of qualities and characteristics that make up the human condition. We realize that life is not simple, but is full of complexities and complications. It becomes harder to decisively place blame since we more readily understand the points of view of multiple sides of contentious issues. That is the advantage of detachment, an attitude that allows us to show more neutrality and fairness, surely a virtue of age.

Sharing Our Stories

As we grow into old age some of us begin to realize how different our growing up years were from those of the youngsters of today. In my mid-seventies there arose in me a desire to record my own story so that my children and grandchildren would have a better picture of my early life. This urge was particularly strong, I think, because the disparities of our life experiences were so marked. I was born in 1928 on a cotton and tobacco farm in North Carolina in a house that had no running water, no central heat, no electricity, and no telephone, and was raised by parents who valued hard work over intellectual achievement. A Bible was the only book in our home. My growing up years took place during the Great Depression, a time of struggle and economic hardship on the farm. When I was two my mother gave birth to a baby boy. Both mother and child came down with German measles, and my baby brother lost his hearing due to the extremely high fever that accompanied the illness. My mother, understandably, became severely depressed, unable to offer the love and nurture so desperately needed by my two-year-old self.

Because of my brother's eventual enrollment in a school for the deaf in St. Louis, I was sent to Washington University with the intention that I would become a teacher of the deaf. But as so often happens, things did not turn out as planned. Much to my Southern Baptist parents' dismay, I fell in love with a young Jewish man who had just returned from serving in the Navy in World War II. After going home for summer break I was told that I would not be allowed to return to school or to the man I loved. I was enraged, so at age eighteen I packed a few summer clothes in a borrowed suitcase and ran away from home. I had no idea where I would live or how I would survive once I arrived in St. Louis. But survive I did, and, with a job as maid and babysitter for a family offering room and board, along with scholarships and student loans, I was able to continue at the university. Norman and I were married before our senior year and graduated together, the first couple in our school to do so. My parents did not acknowledge our wedding or graduation.

I wrote my life story, published it myself, and gave copies to my family on my eightieth birthday. In it I described a way of life that has largely disappeared and retrieved memories that I thought had long ago vanished. As I wrote, I relived some painful experiences, shed many tears, but also recalled occasions that offered important lessons in life. It is my hope that my grandchildren and great-grandchildren will continue to find something of value in reading about not just my early life on a farm but also something of how I developed and matured and what I came to believe and value.

I urge all elders to write or record their life stories, for we owe it to those coming after us. Our heirs will benefit from a knowledge of their heritage and will profit from a sense of generational continuity. If we do not preserve our personal histories, something valuable will be lost forever. Each one of us has interesting, important, meaningful stories to tell; it is up to us to share them.

"More Myself"

In our teen years we are beginning to define who we are, often trying out a variety of behaviors and beliefs. But by our seventies most of us have settled more or less comfortably into ourselves, one notable difference from those earlier years. May Sarton in her book *At Seventy* tells about an encounter she had after a lecture during which she had said, "This is the best time of my life. I love being old." Someone in the audience loudly challenged her: "Why is it good to be old?" Sarton says she was caught off guard and felt a little defensive in the face of the incredulity of her listener. But she replied,

> Because I am more myself than I have ever been. There is less conflict. I am happier, more balanced, and (I heard myself say rather aggressively) "more powerful." I felt it was rather an odd word, "powerful," but I think it is true. It might have been more accurate to say "I am

better able to use my powers." I am surer of what my life
is all about, [and] have less self-doubt to conquer....

Sarton's response tells us that she was aware of the deepening and strengthening of her sense of self, and that this knowledge gave her an awareness of personal power.

Jungian analyst Florida Scott-Maxwell, writing in her eighties, also makes the statement "I am myself as never before," saying that she is herself "with ardour, and no other way seems possible." She indicates, however, that it is not always easy to hold on to this centeredness, writing, "The ordeal of being true to your own inner way must stand high in the list of ordeals. It is like being in the power of someone you cannot reach, know or move, but who never lets you go; who both insists that you accept yourself and who seems to know who you are." From her perspective, settling into ourselves involves both effort and acceptance.

Betty Friedan, who brought us the groundbreaking feminist work *The Feminine Mystique*, later turned her energies toward a study of aging. Friedan was surprised to find "some new dimension of personhood, some strength or quality of being in people who had crossed the chasm of age—and kept on going and growing." She writes of a visit she paid to a friend, a man who in his sixties had been a successful administrator and in his seventies developed a forum for the discussion of public policy in terms of social values. She visited him as he was celebrating his eightieth birthday and found him "so much less heavy and pompous, so warm and witty and wise in the amazing fullness of his age." She quotes from his reflections:

> I'm more and more myself. But I'm more comfortable
> with differences, not uptight about them. I suppose
> along the way I got a larger vision, somehow.... I'm not
> envious of anybody else and I'm not anguished about
> my own failures. I also know if I were there again I'd fail
> again, so what.

This is a man who has come to embrace what he calls "a larger vision" of himself and accepts the totality of his being.

In *Memories, Dreams, Reflections,* written when he was in his early eighties, Jung reflected on the course his life had taken. He said that fundamentally he was satisfied, but that though many things worked out as he had planned, they did not necessarily prove of benefit. He comments:

> But almost everything developed naturally and by destiny. I regret many follies which sprang from my obstinacy; but without that trait I would not have reached my goal. I am astonished, disappointed, pleased with myself. I am distressed, depressed, rapturous.... I exist on the foundation of something I do not know. In spite of uncertainties, I feel a solidity underlying all existence and a continuity in my mode of being.

Jung was acknowledging those attributes which provided him a sense of durability and vitality, of being true to himself.

As we grow old, we learn to be comfortable with our faults and failures, knowing full well that none of us lives without them, that, in fact they have contributed valuable lessons and have enriched our lives. In our seventies we have mostly achieved what we set out to do or have accepted our inability to reach those goals. We realize that our shortcomings and disappointments along with our achievements and satisfactions have made us more human and have made us who we are.

Defining Our Character

This sense of being more ourselves can be thought of as a recognition of our particular personality or character. James Hillman in his book *Force of Character* writes eloquently about the central importance of character in the aging process. Hillman contends that as we live longer, we deepen and strengthen what he defines as "that specific composition of traits, foibles, delights, and commitments, that identifiable figure bearing our name, our history, and a face that mirrors a 'me.'" Character used in this sense does not refer to the presence or absence of moral virtues but rather represents an amalgamation of those attributes that allows us to navigate the complexities of the world in our own unique manner.

Throughout our lives each of us accumulates a particular combination of disappointments and triumphs, vices and virtues, cruelties and kindnesses, joys and sorrows which taken together make us who we are. As so many of us have found, part of that continuing development and learning is in accepting those innermost characteristics that we so often denied or denigrated when we were younger and striving to present ourselves as unflappable, infallible, and invulnerable.

By our seventies we have lived long enough to forge our oddities and our conventionalisms—these disparate and sometimes contradictory qualities—into a more or less coherent whole. We can begin to see all of our characteristics as demonstrations of our selfhood. Hillman reminds those of us at this stage of life that "Your mental capacities and physical vitality may decline in old age, as might your mobility weaken, yet your character shows ever more energy as your form becomes more actualized." It is encouraging to think that as some of our faculties are fading, others are gathering strength.

Hillman sees this energy as an active force, the primary feature of aging. The gerontologist Gene Cohen has a similar perspective, comparing this energy found in elders to the "springtime sap rising through the myriad channels and pores inside a tree, propelling its flowering and seasonal growth." Cohen describes what he calls *developmental intelligence* as the degree to which a person has manifested his or her singular neurological, emotional, intellectual, and psychological capabilities. It is also the process by which these elements become optimally integrated in the mature brain. More specifically, developmental intelligence, as Cohen views it, reflects the maturing synergy of cognition, emotional intelligence, judgment, social skills, life experience, and consciousness. It is the flowering of our individuality, the expression of our character, the shaping of our image, and one of the fascinating and commendable aspects of old age.

The life force within each of us, expressed through character or personality or developmental intelligence, is similar to *entelechy*, the realization of potential. It is variously known as fate or destiny or calling, making us think of an acorn that holds within itself the capacity and promise of becoming a giant oak. Each of us has a uniqueness that is present from the very beginning of our lives. Just as the majesty of the oak emerges from within the tiny acorn, or as the sap rises within the tree to promote its growth, so there is within each of us some form of energy that propels us onto our natural path and urges us onward. I have often imagined the existence of an invisible yet powerfully strong thread that in some mysterious way unwinds and pulls us toward our personal fulfillment. Perhaps it was this strong thread that tugged at my being, giving me the courage to run away from home at age eighteen—and that continues to tug me forward as I live into very old age.

The story of my seventies is an example of what Cohen means when he talks about the age at which we can cultivate and integrate many of our formerly unrecognized and underdeveloped capacities. Going back to school at age sixty-nine gave me the opportunity to explore intellectual abilities that had lain dormant in my early life. Dealing with the dreadful, life-threatening disease of a daughter and the decline and death of my husband were also profoundly formative experiences, reinforcing formerly underdeveloped emotional potentialities that had awaited my years of maturity.

These extremes of remarkable fulfillment and immense sorrow seem to be typical of this stage of life and certainly contribute to the formation of our character and to our further growth as individuals. In many ways, I did not fully become my true self until I had lived through those happy, sorrowful, rewarding, frustrating years. A reinforced, more highly developed sense of self, whenever and however it appears, is a great gift.

Agelessness

Though we have settled into ourselves, learned much from our experiences, come to terms with our circumstances, and established our fundamental character, nevertheless we have a solid sense that we are still much the same as before. As Scott-Maxwell wrote in her eighties, "Life has changed me greatly, it has improved me greatly, but it has also left me practically the same." Our essential personhood or character persists in spite of the difficulties and challenges we encounter as we pursue our path through life. Those of us who have lived enough years begin to see common themes in our life stories and can sometimes catch glimpses of the interior psychological structures that have been revealed in our long histories and complex personalities.

It seems paradoxical that though we continue to grow and learn throughout our later years, we also in some fundamental way remain unchanged. Most of us, regardless of age, have a strong sense of a continuity of self, an agelessness, as if we have always been this same person, even though our appearance and our circumstances may have changed dramatically over the years. We know that we are old, but something within us still feels essentially young or lacking an easily defined age. I know that when I am with younger friends I often forget our age difference. It is as if I am their peer, thinking that we have similar issues and outlooks, and sometimes of course we do, but I doubt they overlook our age disparity so readily.

It is intriguing to think about just what it is that endures throughout all our lives that identifies us as unique. As we have grown from childhood to adulthood, all our cells have been replaced numerous times; our bodies have been stretched and padded as we have added years; our brains have been altered as we have learned new things and forgotten others; our emotional lives have changed as we have suffered failures and celebrated successes. Yet there is some inner blueprint, some inherent pattern that forms us and maintains our particular physical structure and psychological configuration.

That structure might be defined as the extraordinary intertwining of our body and psyche. We most often think of ourselves and others in terms of outer appearance, but the way we look is to a considerable extent a manifestation of inner attitudes and beliefs. The psyche expresses itself through touch, facial expressions, gestures, stance, posture, and gait. While some of these, especially movements, begin to change as our bodies age, others reveal our most distinctive features. Do we habitually smile or frown, shuffle or stride, reach out or withdraw? Though the surface of our being, our outward appearance, does change over time, there remains a consistency in our overall demeanor that sets us apart, divulging the truth of our being, contributing to the sense of self undefined by age alone.

~

Cohen, Gene D. *The Mature Mind: The Positive Power of the Aging Brain.* Cambridge, MA: Basic Books, 2005.

Friedan, Betty. *The Fountain of Age.* New York: Simon & Schuster, 1993.

Hillman, James. *The Force of Character and the Lasting Life.* New York: Random House, 1999.

Jung, C. G. *Memories, Dreams, Reflections.* Rev. ed. Recorded and edited by Aniela Jaffé. Trans. by Richard and Clara Winston. New York: Vintage Books, 1989.

Jung, C. G. "On the Psychology of the Unconscious," *The Collected Works of C. G. Jung,* vol. 7. Ed. and trans. Gerard Adler and R. F. C. Hull. Princeton, NJ: Princeton University Press, 1953.

Sarton, May. *At Seventy: A Journal.* New York: Norton, 1984.

Scott-Maxwell, Florida. *The Measure of My Days.* New York: Penguin, 1968.

The Solace of Solitude

*Loneliness expresses the pain of being alone and solitude
expresses the glory of being alone.*

Paul Tillich
The Courage to Be

Living Alone

It was not until my late seventies that I experienced what it means to live
alone. After I ran away from home at age eighteen, I lived for a while with
a wealthy family as a part-time live-in maid, making it possible for me to
continue in school. Norman and I were finally able to marry in the fall of
1948, a few weeks after I turned twenty, and just before we entered our
senior year at Washington University. That was possible because my
husband's brother generously offered us a tiny room in their modest
house. In return we cooked the evening meals and babysat their two
children. Following graduation we began our own long years of married
family life, including graduate school, then eventually adding two
daughters to our household.

After becoming adjusted to decades of togetherness, in the later stages of
life many of us are likely to find ourselves living alone, perhaps for the
first time. Children have long ago departed for their own homes, and
mates have moved to nursing homes or died. What are we to do? How
are we to handle such a huge change in our daily routine, the absence of
intimacy, the lack of someone with shared experience, the sudden shift of

all household and financial responsibilities to our shoulders? For those of us unaccustomed to aloneness, such a state can at first seem daunting, even frightening. We wonder how we will function or even find ourselves within our solitariness. All too often our identities have been so tightly tied to our partners that we must find new ways to define who we are as persons without companions.

One thing I have learned is that we can feel intensely lonely even when we live with others, and, conversely, we can discover enormous contentment when we no longer share our households. I have now had more than a decade to explore the advantages and disadvantages of living alone and have come to realize that there are different kinds of aloneness, some much more difficult or damaging than others. It is important to distinguish among what I see as the differing states of isolation, loneliness, and solitude.

Isolation

There is potential danger in too much aloneness. Isolation is what we fear most: the prospect of being cut off from human contact, with no one to hear our cries for help, feeds feelings of desolation and abandonment. There are also times when we are not able or willing to voice or even acknowledge our need for and dependence on others. Such inaccessibility can be due to severe depression, when we are emotionally paralyzed, unable to reach out or to act on our own behalf.

I experienced that kind of emotional isolation frequently in my younger life. In those depressive states the image that arose in my mind was myself as a small child, curled in a fetal position, lying in the bottom of a deep well, a place where no one could hear me or reach me. It was not so much a feeling of fear but of being neglected, deserted; I felt I had been cast off into a lifeless, dark, dank hellhole, deprived of human contact. Most disturbing was the sense that no one cared, the certainty that no effort would be made to rescue me. Fortunately, that despairing image no longer haunts me, but I shall always remember that dreadful sense of desolation and abandonment—utter, unrelenting isolation. It is a state of mind, and of situation, to be avoided if at all possible.

We can also become isolated because of infirmity or physical impairment. When we are no longer capable of getting around on our own, our immobility may make maintaining connection with others extremely difficult. Being confined to a wheelchair can certainly feel isolating, especially when much-needed assistance is not readily available. Occasionally the sense of isolation is because we are too ill, lacking the strength or capacity to ask for help. If we know persons in these circumstances, it is important to reach out to them and offer our presence as well as practical support.

Another kind of isolation comes when we lose our hearing. Some of us find it hard to admit that we can no longer hear well, for unlike a need for glasses due to fading eyesight, a loss of hearing that requires the use of hearing aids carries some social stigma and may therefore add to a diminished sense of self. When of necessity we resort to hearing aids, we are often assaulted by unreasonably, near unbearably, loud surroundings (as in many restaurants), which makes us wish to avoid such places. Since I have a hearing loss myself, I have frequently felt frustrated when I am in a noisy environment or with a large group enthusiastically engaged in conversation, talking over one another, laughing loudly. At such times, when communication becomes difficult, it is tempting to recede into ourselves, become withdrawn and resentful. I try mightily to resist that pull to disengage, for it is our connectedness that sustains us. In spite of the challenges, we need to maintain our relationships, for they are crucial to our well-being.

Without human contact we can become hardened and shriveled from lack of the nourishment that comes from interaction with others. We know that long periods of isolation or extreme sensory deprivation can cause intellectual deterioration, increased suggestibility, and in some cases, hallucinations. Even in less extreme situations, surely we do not wish to look back on our lives realizing that we cut ourselves off from that which feeds us emotionally and psychologically. It is important to send a short email or make a phone call to keep in touch with family and friends. A quiet lunch or dinner at home with friends who are willing to help with provisions may be one way to avoid noisy environments while remaining in touch with others. It is wise to remember that isolation, whatever its cause, is often damaging and can be deadly.

Loneliness

Whereas isolation is a peril to be avoided when possible, loneliness is of a different order; it is usually less threatening. It might be the emptiness we feel following a separation, a divorce, or when our children go off to school for the first time—or later when they leave to live their own lives elsewhere. Loneliness can plague us even when we are in the presence of others. For me, it wasn't living alone but rather the tantalizing closeness yet undeniable distance created by my husband's illness that brought on my most poignant loneliness.

When Norman was slowly declining into dementia, our ability to bridge the chasm of communication was seriously impaired. Though we shared a home and bed, sat next to each other and chatted, we rarely had any significant or thoughtful dialogue. I felt as if I were speaking to an empty shell, his mind having departed, leaving his body behind. The bond of family, the memories of almost sixty years of marriage, and the common emotional and intellectual life were all but destroyed by the plaques and tangles that had overtaken his brain. We talked, but he was unable to deal with complexities or grasp subtleties, so our conversations were limited and repetitive; they lacked the stimulation of genuine exchange. During those times, though his body was present, I felt an unspeakable loneliness.

A similar experience of loneliness occurs when we are in a group that does not share our perspective or is not interested in the ideas that are most important to us. We may hold views, political or religious or philosophical, that are not acceptable, or have a lifestyle that is not congruent with that of the group. We may feel we know more than those around us about topics being discussed but are uncomfortable in expressing our opinions for fear of being thought arrogant or conceited. Many of us have had the experience of being in a large social gathering only to find ourselves intensely lonely. We are aware of a world out there, but it seems to recede from us; we feel unable to penetrate it or to become a part of it. The feeling of being disconnected, without heartfelt discourse, is uncomfortable, but that discomfort creates a strong desire to come back into relationship, to re-enter community. We may feel removed from some others, but we still wish to be a part of the human circle.

I am reminded of the words of the theologian John Dunne, who in noting the human condition, talks about the longing in loneliness, what he calls "the heart's desire." He suggests that "to know the human heart, it seems, we must go out to meet our loneliness in solitude, and then we must come back again to meet it in the human circle." Loneliness is a state in which connections exist but are temporarily missing or distorted. There are other people somewhere, but we cannot reach them.

Thomas Dumm, in *Loneliness as a Way of Life*, suggests that such words as *exiled, untouched, ignored, isolated, desolated, alienated, outcast, denied, lost, mad* summarize what many of us feel when we are in a place where we, at least temporarily, are not easily touched by others. For some of us it is emotionally painful to be alone for long periods of time. We are bereft, lost, impoverished; we are in a state of near despair, feel a creeping dread of deep isolation. We have not yet reached the understanding that with solitude can come an opportunity to become more fully who we truly are and can help us develop a renewed sense of self-reliance.

Solitude

I learned about solitude when my husband moved to a residential facility for Alzheimer's patients. Though I had already taken over all the household chores and financial obligations, I still wondered how I would manage living completely alone. Surprisingly, after a few weeks I learned that living by myself did not necessarily mean feeling lonelier than I had felt when he was at home. When asked by friends how I was faring, I was reluctant at first to admit how good it was to have the house to myself, fearing that I would be betraying my ailing husband. Partly, of course, my positive reaction was that I no longer had the daily physical responsibility of caring for him; but the exhilaration I felt was not just from the relief of having much of that load lifted from my shoulders. It was also a newly discovered freedom—an ability to set my own schedule, to determine my own priorities, to focus on my own needs. Though I was living alone, I was not lonely. I had discovered that in contrast to isolation and loneliness, there is comfort and benefit, indeed solace, offered by solitude.

Anthony Storr, author and psychiatrist, tells us that traditional psychotherapists consider the ability to form healthy relationships a fundamental criterion of emotional maturity. While that is certainly true, he points out that the capacity to be alone, since it has to do with self-discovery and self-realization, is equally important in psychic development. Solitude is a time, Storr says, to become "aware of one's deepest needs, feelings, and impulses." This kind of awareness is particularly valuable for older persons, though many find it beneficial earlier in life.

Persons who have extraordinary gifts of creativity, such as scientists, artists, writers, and musicians, often choose to spend prolonged periods of time alone in their labs or studios. They find their greatest visions and discoveries come when they can allow their imaginations free rein without interruption. In the same manner, many great religious leaders have taken extended periods of solitude during which they gathered insights and revelations that they brought back to share with the world. We all benefit from those who have learned to value and to make good use of their times alone.

That same opportunity for self-discovery and self-examination makes solitude welcome as we enter our later years. In addition to relief at being excused from burdensome responsibilities, for many of us encroaching age brings a greater desire for introspection and contemplation. We feel a need for a limited kind of withdrawal, a distancing from what once were our normal interactions with others. We find value and deep satisfaction in having time alone to think and reflect. We relish the opportunity to come to terms with just who we are and how we fit into the world. It is a time for meditation, for looking inward, for what I think of as the in-gathering of our soul's work.

Solitude and the Essential Self

Carol Ochs, writing on women and spirituality, sees the quest for solitude as a desire to escape what society demands of us in order to discover what she calls "our essential self." For her, solitude is the ability to comfortably accept the absence of external contacts, whereas loneliness indicates an inability to be content with such absence. We may be lonely due to our own refusal to touch or be touched by others, while we can be happy in solitude because we are more deeply in touch with ourselves.

Alice Koller, in her book *The Stations of Solitude*, examines philosophical and personal aspects of this subject. She uses the metaphor of journey, and though her inner journey appears similar to a spiritual quest, Koller disclaims any religious intent. She writes that solitude is for her a moral and intellectual pursuit concerned with clarifying and bringing together "into one consistent whole what would otherwise be the erratically joined parts of my mind and my actions, each within each, each to each. The philosopher I am is inextricably entwined with the person I am." Koller's search for wholeness in solitude is a process familiar to introverts, who are primarily sustained and bolstered by quiet times alone.

Jung coined the phrases *introvert* and *extravert* to refer to two temperaments or psychological types. Among other differences, extraverts are energized by being among people while introverts find themselves replenished by being alone. To be either extreme is to risk descending into neurosis, but most of us fall somewhere along the middle portion of the spectrum. Though those of us who are introverts seek and enjoy human companionship, we often find ourselves depleted by being with too many people or even a single person for too long a time. We seek ways to stay involved while keeping our social activities to a manageable level. As Florida Scott-Maxwell notes, "the liveliness of companionship and the liveliness of solitude differ, and the latter is never as exhausting as the former." When alone we can respond unreservedly to our bodily needs and rhythms. I appreciate those times when I can indulge myself, satisfy my appetite with cookies and milk or a glass of wine, comfort my body with a warm bath or a nap, and fulfill my desire for quiet. It feels good to answer to no one save myself.

Scott-Maxwell further comments that often we need the absence of others in order to fully appreciate and enjoy what she calls the "magic of things." She wonders if living alone makes us more alive. With too much togetherness we endanger our ability to absorb the beauty and evanescent quality of our surroundings. With solitude we can take time to observe, to reflect, to rest and care for ourselves—and as a result, to be more alive. I agree with her, for I find that I appreciate the beauty of my garden and the comfort of my home most when I am alone, able to focus on my deep connection to my surroundings. The aloneness allows a shift of awareness to take place.

Another kind of change in mental outlook is required during bereavement. In old age we are likely to face the deaths of dear friends or a life partner. Sometimes in an effort to come to terms with the pain and suffering of our loss we seek distractions by increasing our social contacts or by continuing to engage in everyday busyness. We are told that we need social interaction to calm our distress and assuage our sorrow. Being with emotionally supportive friends is important and can indeed be helpful, but solitude may turn out to be the most therapeutic way to deal with overwhelming grief. After all, it is during times alone that we can best recall and mourn those deeply private and intimate experiences with the deceased.

At a recent lunch with a ninety-five-year-old friend, we talked about what solitude has brought to our lives. She said that she had never been introspective and had never been interested in discovering what she called "her true self." But in her later years, living alone, she said she had spent more and more time looking inward, thinking about what might be called her essential self. Her experience of increased contemplation and self-analysis, what might be called soul-searching, parallels that of many of my aging friends. Old age does somehow compel us to examine our innermost selves in ways we had not had time nor inclination for in our younger years.

Solitude and Balance

May Sarton comments on her fear of being alone in her book *Journal of a Solitude*: "The ambiance here is order and beauty. That is what frightens me when I am first alone again. I feel inadequate. I have made an open place, a place for meditation. What if I cannot find myself inside it?" Her struggle with balancing her need for companionship with her equally strong desire to preserve for herself space and time for the expression of her wholeness often filled her with anxiety. As she puts it, "It occurs to me that boredom and panic are the two devils the solitary must combat. When I lay down this afternoon, I could not rest and finally got up because I was in a sweat of panic, panic for no definable reason, a panic of solitude, I presume." But in spite of her momentary panic, Sarton continued to live alone.

Just as a balance between introversion and extraversion is desirable, so for Sarton living comfortably alone demanded a level of what she calls *poise*. She points out that when we live alone we always have room for a stranger or for a new friend. At the same time our need for aloneness must not be sacrificed in our wish to be always open and receptive. She acknowledges that being alone can be difficult but that for her being with others without a period of solitude is even worse. Without solitude, she says, she loses her center, feels "dispersed, scattered, in pieces." As she says, it all comes back to poise, the poise of the soul in true balance. Perhaps that is why we cherish solitude in our old age: it gives us the opportunity to gather our scattered pieces and bind them together to form some meaningful view of our lives.

What is needed when we live alone is the equivalent of Sarton's balance or poise or Dunne's alternate withdrawals and returns, which, he says, can lead us to expect "our heart's desire to kindle in solitude, and when it has kindled, to illumine all the roads of life." That is, the experience of solitude can be life-expanding and life-enriching by both allowing us an opportunity for self-exploration and then by drawing us back into relationship. It would serve us well to remember that the boundaries we draw as we express our need for solitude can both serve as protection against unwanted encroachment on our privacy as well as exclude opportunities for relationship. It is essential that we find a way of weaving together and unraveling the threads of the opposing needs for solitude and for connection. Both are necessary for a life of harmony and equilibrium.

Solitude as Anchor

Recently I read about anchorites, Catholic religious hermits who during the Middle Ages took vows to remain in one place. They often lived in small cells attached to a church. Just as a ship is stabilized in place when it drops its anchor, the community's place of worship was "anchored" by these dedicated servants of God. The anchorites did not leave their cells, but could hear Mass and receive Holy Communion through small windows facing the sanctuary. In each cell there was another small window through which supplies were received and through which spiritual advice was offered to those in need. These solitary figures came to acquire a reputation for wisdom. One of the most famous anchorites was Julian of Norwich, a woman (referred to as an anchoress) whose writings have had a great and lasting impression on Christian spirituality. She did not believe in a wrathful God who punished sinners, and she wrote texts comparing Jesus to Mother, a controversial perspective then and now.

I am less interested in such beliefs than in the concept of *anchor*. *Stability of place* can be thought of in metaphorical terms. As old people we serve as anchors for our families. Our times of solitude allow us to embody stability of place because we carry within us the weight of our family's history, its stories, its characteristics, its successes and failures. If we have established our role as respected elder—matriarch or patriarch—it is with us that the family vessel remains securely moored. We have lived long enough to be firmly centered in ourselves and perhaps have accrued enough wisdom that we can help others remain grounded. Our anchoring provides a sense of safety and security for family and friends who seek continuity and connection with one another.

We can also help stabilize our communities. Some of us hold the knowledge of our community's past and can serve as anchors of remembrance, recalling what is no longer present. We know what used to be there, how things used to look, what used to be done, and how things have changed. There is value in such information; it benefits us see where our communities have made progress and where they have failed. Community leaders can learn from its oldest and wisest inhabitants what policies have worked and which have not and why.

Though the anchorites did not take vows of silence, they spent most of their time in silent prayer. It is in silence that we find ourselves most able to reconstitute and consolidate our memories and reflections into a solid, durable framework that anchors us and allows us to be examples of emotional, psychological, and spiritual stability for our loved ones. When we are alone, as Sarton says, we are less scattered, less distracted, more centered, more *anchored*. In my solitude, there is no needless chatter, no intrusion upon my voluntary seclusion. I can bask in the tranquility that comes with an absence of noise.

In my years of living alone I have found solitude to be much more comforting and rewarding than I had imagined. Unlike loneliness or isolation, solitude provides an opportunity for renewal and revitalization. By spending time without the demands or presence of others we can indulge in the pleasures of reminiscing, reflecting, and ruminating. We can collect and recollect our thoughts and look inward rather than focusing on outward events. While alone we can spend time in productive examination of the self, a pastime we are more and more inclined to indulge in during our later years and something that brings its own rewards. Solitude is one of the gifts of growing old.

$\sim$

Dumm, Thomas. *Loneliness as a Way of Life.* Cambridge, MA: Harvard University Press, 2008.

Dunne, John S. *The Reasons of the Heart: A Journey into Solitude and Back Again into the Human Circle.* Notre Dame: University of Notre Dame Press, 1978.

Koller, Alice. *The Stations of Solitude.* New York: William Morrow, 1990.

Ochs, Carol. *Women and Spirituality.* Totowa, NJ: Rowman & Allanheld, 1983.

Sarton, May. *Journal of a Solitude.* New York: Norton, 1973.

Scott-Maxwell, Florida. *The Measure of My Days.* New York: Penguin, 1968.

Storr, Anthony. *Solitude: A Return to the Self.* New York: Ballantine, 1988.

Tillich, Paul. *The Courage to Be.* New Haven: Yale University Press, 1952.

Eighty—Age of Fulfillment

I think instead [of happiness] we should be working for contentment...an inner sense of fulfillment that's relatively independent of external circumstances.

Andrew Weil
Healthy Aging

Reaching Eighty

When on my eightieth birthday I was asked to make a wish as I blew out the (eight) candles on my cake, I was unexpectedly rendered speechless. It struck me that I had nothing to wish for; at that extraordinary moment I had everything I needed or wanted, was completely satisfied, fulfilled. A strange feeling of *absence of want* seeped into me slowly over the next weeks and months. I began to realize that the primary objectives of my life—seen more clearly in retrospect, of course—had largely been achieved. My basic physical and emotional needs had been met, my modest ambitions attained, and many of my fondest dreams realized. I felt loved and appreciated. I had a deep sense of contentment and completion.

This rather self-satisfied daze was followed by a surprising thought: If I were to drop dead at this very moment, all would be fine! I would have no major regrets, no unfinished business, no pangs of guilt. At first that insight brought a feeling of utter relief, for in the past I had often obsessed over some lapse in judgment or failure in relationship, had repeatedly agonized over important and not-so-important decisions, and had frequently been burdened by guilt over what I perceived to be inexcusable mistakes or troubled by gross stupidities. As all those real and imagined shortcomings faded into insignificance, it was as if a weight had been lifted from my shoulders and a binding loosened from around my heart. I felt free, could breathe more easily.

I had barely assimilated that feeling of freedom, however, when I was struck by another startling realization: Something profound had come to an end. My life of yearning and striving was over. A sense of imminent endings loomed over me, casting a chilling shadow on my initial elation. All those needs and desires in my early life had pushed me forward, provided me with enthusiasm and purpose. If they are no longer present, what would give me incentive for my remaining time on this earth? Did the absence of want suggest I was finished with life? That possibility brought a flash of anxiety. On the one hand, it seemed unreasonable, for I was still in good health. On the other hand, I was entering what was certain to be the final stage of my life; I could sense the end approaching. Yet I continued to find great joy and fulfillment in my activities and in time spent with my family and friends. (And, additionally, thinking seriously about what it means to grow old.) Perhaps it is just this ability to face the inevitability of death while still finding pleasure in everyday life that sustains us and allows us to live fully in spite of our advanced age.

When I reached age eighty-five I was overwhelmed with a sense of gratefulness and liveliness, even exhilaration, at having lived to this ripe old age. As a means of expressing my delight, I wrote a bit of doggerel titled "Eighty-Five" and sent it to my family and friends.

> Wow! I have reached age eighty-five!
> And am absolutely thrilled to be alive!
> Along with a case of eight-five-itis,
> I have a bit of osteoarthritis,
> also have endured a bout of colitis,

and even suffered from sinusitis,
though understandably escaped prostatitis.

Still, living to be so very, very old
has brought me gifts dear to behold,
and has made me eager to uphold
my desire to be a most worthy mold
for those whose lives continue to unfold.

Amazingly enough, I keep on growing,
learning to be more loving and outgoing,
attempting deeper awareness and self-knowing
as I contemplate the hoped-for showing
of courage as my life rolls to its final slowing.

Until that time of my sure demise
I shall never cease to emphasize
how important it is to recognize
that life is always capable of surprise,
and that eventually I must say my goodbyes.

But for now, man, oh man, I am eighty-five!
And mighty happy to be alive.

That joyful sentiment continues to live within me as I approach ninety.

Old Old Age

It is not easy to admit to frailties, to acknowledge faltering energy or
failing memory. These alterations in our bodies and brains tell us that we
are going through a transition, that we are perhaps feeling the downward
pull of a late-life drop into a deeper level of consciousness. If we recognize
the signs, we can learn from these changes and benefit from allowing a
meaningful transformation to take place. That is what transition is all

about: watching the old self merge with newer attributes—changed and yet remaining the same.

Instead of accepting these changes, we may be inclined to fight against them, trying to maintain a physically active life that is no longer appropriate for our aging bodies. This kind of heroic mindset is widespread in our culture with its emphasis on acting and looking young. It is not that physical activity is to be avoided; prudent exercise has been shown to be extremely important in maintaining healthy bodies and minds. But for most of us, striving for the same pace of vigorous activity that we pursued when we were younger only betrays fear and desperation. There are gains to be had from acknowledging our aging and finding the benefits of a slower, more deliberative lifestyle. We can, as has been recommended, pay more attention to our soul's work, solidifying our relationships, addressing unresolved matters with others and within ourselves, and preparing for our ultimate stage of life.

This has been mentioned before, but perhaps it is worth repeating that it is important to remember that though our bodies may weaken and our memories fade, our fundamental selfhood can be strengthened as we age, for it is not dependent upon physical agility or youthful appearance, but rather is a manifestation of the continued growth of our uniqueness. If we attend to it, the inner core of our being can be reinforced rather than diminished as we grow old. The knowledge of that continued development can sustain us and make our later years fruitful and meaningful. As I moved from my mid-eighties into my late eighties, I was increasingly aware that I am well past middle old age and am entering that stage of life called by gerontologists "old old age." This is a sobering time in which I think more deeply than ever about my past—remembering those I have loved, some of whom have preceded me in death; recalling work I enjoyed or endured; recollecting accomplishments that give me a measure of pride; and reviewing actions and behaviors that I wish I had avoided. On one level I am awaiting my demise, while at a deeper level I am continually in the process of discovering who I really am.

In addition to reminiscing and reflecting on the lives we've lived, at this late stage we may seriously consider how to best spend the time that is left to us. If we have not done so before, then it is a reminder to get our affairs in order, share advance directives or living wills, and make appropriate arrangements for our heirs. We might initiate discussions with our friends and family regarding wishes for end-of-life care and preferences for funeral (or memorial service) and burial. We may decide to spend more time and offer more loving attention to those we care about, thereby making peace with others and ourselves.

Another way of communicating our legacy, how we wish to be remembered, is by writing an ethical will, a document expressing our beliefs and values, which may include messages or advice for our family and friends (described in detail in Chapter 8, under "The Well-Planned Exit"). Some of us may also find composing a eulogy for ourselves a helpful exercise, helping us reach a deeper understanding of the patterns of behavior and belief that have contributed to the course of our lives. I have come to appreciate more deeply my painful experiences for I now understand how they contributed to my empathy and compassion, how they helped me identify more fully with the suffering of others. This inner work can bring on a feeling of release, fulfillment, and serenity as a profound sense of gratitude washes over us for all we have experienced during our lives.

In an earlier chapter I mentioned the importance of telling our stories, so if we have not done it before, now might be the time to offer our families the gift of our own life history. We can talk to our children and grandchildren, perhaps allowing them to record our remembrances, or for those of us who have the inclination, as I did, to create a personal history. Writing my autobiography helped me make sense of my life, for in the process I discovered many memories that had been hidden and thought lost but which came to light as my story unfolded on the page. Whatever the means, I strongly recommend that we find ways to share our stories.

To summarize, for those of us among the "oldest old" the final phase of our lives can be a time of discovery. The lessons to be learned are varied, from wisdom gained, to deepened compassion as a result of serious illness, to enduring the loss of a mate or good friends, as well as encountering unexpected adventures, forming new friendships, and reaching a greater understanding of what it means to be alive.

Coming to Terms

Those of us over eighty-five now constitute the fastest-growing sector of our population. If we have lived this long, we have an average life expectancy of perhaps another decade, with a distinct possibility of living to be one hundred. Along with our good fortune at reaching this advanced age, the probability is that we will be called on to make many major life adjustments. It is time for us to come to terms with the changes that may be ahead.

Old age is often characterized as a time of adamant resistance to change, and of course that is sometimes the way we react to unwelcome transitions. Since we are likely to be faced with failing energy, having to leave our home, or being forced to relinquish our cherished independence, there is perhaps no other stage of life during which we are required to make so many extreme alterations in our habitual way of living. Part of the discomfort or depression we experience is likely due to our very resistance. We understandably chafe at our illnesses or physical limitations and having to depend on children or younger friends in ways that upend our roles. We may fail to recognize the damaging demands placed on our loved ones when we refuse to admit our need for the kind of care that can only be had in residential facilities or nursing homes.

Many of us make these adjustments with open hearts and minds, accepting the reality of our circumstances. In general, we elders are much more flexible and resilient than we are given credit for. We have already lived through numerous stages of life and have learned to accept change, to tolerate ambiguity, and to cope with paradox. It must be acknowledged, however, that some of us find learning to lean on others especially difficult; admitting a need for help erodes our sense of independence. Our culture values a stouthearted, individualistic attitude, so our inclination is to insist that we can still take care of ourselves, that we have no need to rely on others. Given this superhuman expectation, a call for assistance indicates weakness.

But dependence versus independence is a false duality. Our entire lives are spent depending on one another in any number of ways. Interdependence is how we truly function in family and community. We were cared for, and we cared for others. As we decline physically and perhaps mentally, we may be forced to admit that we lack the level of competence that we formerly had. Recognizing our increasing dependency and accepting it as a necessary aspect of aging can in fact be liberating: *I am free to accept what I need.* If we have spent our lives giving to others, then it seems only fitting that in our later years we learn how to gracefully receive. The fact is, no matter the stage of life, we survive only through interdependence, giving to others and receiving from others as the situation requires.

As mentioned before, and in spite of the possibility of these drastic changes in our lives, as a group we are healthier and wealthier than any previous generation, so many of us in our eighties and nineties still maintain a sizable store of vitality, both physical and mental. Most of us, having retired from careers and finished with parental responsibilities, will have the leisure to pursue new experiences and form new relationships. Modern technology allows us to maintain contact easily and often with family members and friends, and most communities offer special programs of interest to the elderly, keeping us informed of current events and socially involved.

Many of us will continue living alone with some outside help. As we come to terms with accepting whatever assistance we need, one of our greatest assets as we live into our ultimate years is our self-assurance, which is supported by remaining as involved and engaged as we can. That is expressed in this verse from the poem "For the Interim Time" by John O'Donohue:

> As far as you can, hold your confidence.
> Do not allow confusion to squander
> This call which is loosening
> Your roots in false ground,
> That you might come free
> From all you have outgrown.

Strengthening spiritual beliefs and pursuing inner work such as mindful meditation or other contemplative practices help affirm our fundamental authenticity and maintain the essence of our character. If we are still uncertain about who we are and what we believe, then this stage of life might be a good time to reflect on those questions—to examine our basic values, explore what it means to be authentic, and scrutinize our behavior to be certain that it best reflects how we wish to be remembered.

Letting Go

In Chapter 3, I wrote about the significance of developing patience, acceptance, and detachment. Those qualities continue to be of importance, but as we live into our eighties, detachment morphs into an even more profound *letting go*.

One of the things we must let go of is our youthful perception of ourselves. We learn to look at our aging bodies—not as objects of derision or embarrassment, but as vessels that have, for the most part, served us well even though we have sometimes been careless, even harsh, in our treatment of them. Like beloved but fragile cups that we have used for decades, we must now handle our old bodies with gentle, loving care. We can show respect by giving extra attention to those stiff knees and shoulders or arthritic fingers and by expressing appreciation for their good service over the years. Our bodies may become worn out, ill, or disabled, but then we must remember that our physical selves are only the worldly containers of our essence, which is something else again.

For those of us who have held demanding jobs in business or education or who have devoted ourselves to professional or artistic careers requiring intense involvement with our work, there may be great difficulty in letting go of the personal identities that have given us recognition and satisfaction through the years we devoted to our occupations. We may continue to think of ourselves primarily as teachers, lawyers, physicians, CEOs, hairdressers, painters, musicians, or laborers, long past the time when those identities describe our present circumstances. We suffer if we persist in identifying with a sense of self that is no longer applicable for our stage of life. Better to let go the old images and find new or more basic foundations for our individualities, ones that reflect more deeply who we are.

There is also a letting go of material goods. One of the great liberations of old age is the decline of acquisitiveness. When young we were most likely victims of and enthusiastic participants in our consumerist society, collecting things just for the sake of having the latest style or the most up-to-date gadget. But there comes a time when we no longer feel the necessity to own whatever is touted as the most recent must-have object. It is a time not of acquiring but of discarding items no longer serving our real or imagined needs. Getting rid of the no-longer-needed goods accumulated throughout a lifetime poses its own challenge, but one which we would do well to take on. I have enlisted the aid of my adult grandchildren in sorting through which of my personal possessions it is time to get rid of, hoping thereby to simplify the chores of family members I will leave behind. I am also asking each of them to indicate which items of my household are of particular interest to them. I have recorded their preferences so that a fair distribution may be made upon my death.

It is not just material objects that we must let go. I find that I must relinquish any hope of keeping up with much of today's technological advances. We are living through the most rapid increase of technology ever known. It seems hard to believe that I grew up in a rural area without electricity or telephones whereas today virtually everyone has a mobile phone and a computer. Procedures such as navigating the internet and social media that are easy, even intuitive, for my grandchildren and great-grandchildren are often completely baffling to me, so I have learned to acknowledge my ignorance and depend on others for assistance.

I have also given up trying to stay abreast of popular culture, often leaving me feeling a bit discomfited when conversation turns to the latest music groups or celebrities. Again, I must admit to my lack of information (or lack of interest), offering no pretense of being current. No longer coveting the most up-to-date objects and realizing how incompetent many of us are when it comes to modern technology or contemporary tastes in music or fashion can contribute to the inevitable feeling that we are out of touch with the times.

With advanced age there comes not just the sense of being considered old-fashioned, but also the fear of being deemed irrelevant or superfluous. We wonder if we have a legitimate place in the world. Those feelings are exacerbated by the ageism that we often experience, by the frequent reminders that the world really belongs to the young. I would suggest that we remind ourselves and those of the younger generation that those us who are old carry the stories, the knowledge, the history, and experience that only comes with age. It is also incumbent upon us to live our later years in a manner that makes us worthy of respect.

One way of combatting these attitudes is for us elders to cultivate friends of all ages. Cross-generational relationships are enriching and beneficial to all, for we learn to more fully appreciate the issues facing those in all stages of life. One of the most gratifying aspects of my old age is the close bond I have with my adult grandchildren. They visit frequently so I am able to keep tabs on their activities, interests, and perspectives on current events. It also surprises and pleases me that in the past decade I have made many new, intimate friends, all of whom are much younger than I. These new friends are especially valued, for they know and accept me as I am now—and not in the context of my former roles as wife and mother. They also help keep me engaged and informed regarding contemporary views, tastes, and trends.

Slowing Down

Along with *letting go* is the necessity for *slowing down*. Our muscles are not as strong or as flexible, our joints not as pliable or reliable, and our balance not as certain as when we were young. We must accommodate to those changes by slowing down, for falling is one of the greatest hazards of this age group. Too many of us suffer fractured hips and broken bones, so it is essential that we walk carefully, hold on to bannisters when going up and down stairs, and continue to maintain whatever strength and balance we have by participating in appropriate exercise.

It is not only our bodies that slow down, but our brains also. I am aware that I do not process information as quickly as I once did. I must ask young people, clerks, technicians, or phone representatives to *please speak more slowly*. There is often the necessity to have information repeated more than once so that it can be properly imprinted on my sluggish brain cells. Partly this is due to my impaired hearing, but also is a result of a genuine lagging of the brain's ability to assimilate meaning from a rapidly delivered series of sometimes confusing and unfamiliar words.

And of course there is the problem of memory. There is no question but that our short-term memory fades with age. Proper names seem to be among the first to go. Repeating the name with a determined effort to fixate it in the mind immediately after an introduction helps, but still we sometimes find that the name of someone or something quite familiar seems to have weirdly suddenly disappeared. It's as if a hole in our brain has suddenly opened up allowing the word to drop out, only to possibly reappear at some later time. A daily calendar is essential in keeping track of appointments and obligations. Then we must remember to consult it every day! Post-it notes are an enormous aid for they can be placed wherever we might need a reminder of things to be done. But perhaps the greatest relief comes if we can just admit to our failing memory and ask for whatever help we need in recovering what has been temporarily forgotten.

Celebrations

I have always believed in celebrations. In my household of mixed heritages—my husband was Jewish and I was raised Christian— I attempted to recognize in some way the special holidays of both traditions. I wanted our children to value the fundamental teachings that each of these religions brought to our family. We had a Christmas tree and a menorah and shared Easter dinner and Seder evenings with friends and family. Since we did not belong to any of the established institutions, I began a tradition of organizing and conducting rituals for special family occasions, such as decade birthdays, Thanksgiving, coming-of-age ceremonies for my grandchildren, welcoming the births of great-grandchildren, and many other events that our family observed. By celebrating these occasions in an intimate and secure environment, we found a safe way to share our deepest feelings and thoughts. Such festivities have helped bond our family into a strong, loving, supportive group.

The importance of celebration continues in my old age. I gave a large party at my home for my eightieth birthday and have had many parties and special dinners since that time. There is nothing more fun and nourishing than being surrounded by like-minded individuals who rejoice along with us as we continue our journey through life. Recently some friends who hosted a dinner for the birthday of a friend asked each guest to say what had been her greatest gift to them. It was touching to hear what each person had to say and to hear her response. One of the young men said that she had given him the gift of *hope*. I was reminded of the quotation that opens the next chapter: "Hope is what the competence of elders brings to the dilemmas of the young."

That kind of occasion is something that can and should be paid forward. As a result of that spectacular evening I have decided to do the same kind of party for some of my friends who have reached old age. What better way to help them acknowledge and celebrate their later years than by learning just what they have contributed to the lives of others. And what joy it must bring to the recipient to hear the influence she or he has had on family members and friends.

A Larger Perspective

An essential aspect of gracefully growing old is developing an ability to laugh at our failures and frailties. As I mentioned in Chapter 4, we have an increased sense of detachment, and what once seemed so necessary, so urgent, so frightfully important is now often seen as insignificant, trivial, even frivolous. We can find humor in our former attachments, especially those attitudes that no longer serve us well. Many years ago Norman Cousins discovered the power of laughter when he was in intense pain and told that he was dying. He decided, as a last desperate move, to watch funny movies. He discovered that genuine laughter served as an anesthetic, providing him with much-needed rest. He eventually recovered and wrote about his experience. We would do well to cultivate a similar approach to some of the humiliating aspects of our aging, such as unfortunate leakages or unpleasant emissions—better to laugh than to lament.

If we continue to anticipate positive experiences as we grow old and if we maintain optimism regarding what this ultimate stage of life can do for us, we will be motivated to nurture our capacities for continued growth—mentally, psychologically, and emotionally. If we cultivate a mindset of hope and humor, instead of bemoaning those things we can no longer do, we might celebrate those that we can do, such as figuring out how to best contribute to a changing and improved perspective on aging. We can help create a new vision of what it means to reach for, and live into, the high point of our lives. We can show that we need not dread this ultimate stage, but can view it as an opportunity to be freed from all we have outgrown. We can try to be the best possible example of an old person.

Our decades of studying, working, and living have helped prepare us for this stage of life in countless ways. Though we have made our share of missteps and frequently have had to diverge from our planned way of doing things, we have had the opportunity to learn from those blunders and adjust accordingly. Over the years we have encountered a variety of changing circumstances—personal, cultural, economic—and thus have learned to adapt. Chances are that a spouse or a good friend has died, imbuing us with a sense of acceptance and a depth of sympathy heretofore unexplored or expressed. We have maintained relationships in spite of differences and confrontations, teaching us the value of forgiveness, understanding, and compromise, or we may have learned to separate from others without bitterness.

Because most of us at this age have developed an acute awareness of our mortality, we probably have learned the value of *being* as opposed to *doing*. Though our outer involvements have added to our store of worldly knowledge, it is our inner work that contributes most deeply to our emotional maturity. It is in just *being* that we have an opportunity to widen and deepen our psychological perspective so that we might live into a more meaningful, satisfying, and fulfilling old age.

Late Eighties: A Softening

I am now in my late eighties. I am a widow. I live alone. As I have noted, my hair is gray, my face is lined, my hands are covered with age spots, and my hearing is fading. It is also true that my breasts are sagging, my belly is bulging, my knees are stiff and creaky, my voice is croaky, my back is sore, my fingers are gnarled, my energy is waning, and my memory often fails me. And yet, I can say without reservation that I have never been happier. How can that be? Given the emphasis our culture places on the physical attributes of strength and beauty, I should be disheartened, even deeply depressed. But conventional wisdom, with its focus on old age as a time of decline and debility, misses much of the essence of what it means to grow old. Though as elders we suffer losses in vigor and speed of thought and movement, we stand to gain in the strength of our character and in the power of our capacity to face with calm endurance whatever life has to offer. In many ways I have flourished in my old age. I even took voice lessons in my mid-eighties, finding great pleasure in revisiting old songs that I had enjoyed singing in earlier years. I have grown intellectually, made many new friends, and broadened my contacts and interests. It has been an extraordinarily rich period of my life. And so it can be for anyone who disavows the damaging stereotypes of aging.

Those of us fortunate enough to live long have learned that we are best served when we can refrain from fighting the flow of life. We have learned that we may face bewildering burdens or unanticipated afflictions, but in spite of these trials, life goes on, so we might as well embrace our destiny with as much grace as we can muster. Many of us, by the time we reach our eighties, have learned to navigate the currents of life, giving ourselves over to the ebb and flow while still maintaining our buoyancy and our orientation. We have learned not to move too insistently upstream, against the current; we have learned not to be pulled down by the undertow of discouraging events, but to keep our heads above water—at least most of the time. Throughout our lives we have been taught to swim ahead with determination, to steer our way courageously through rocky rapids, to thrash around vigorously when some imagined danger threatens. Later we discover that it is often to our advantage to let go, to just gently, fearlessly, float. The older we get, it seems, the easier the floating becomes. We have learned the importance of giving ourselves over to the natural flow of our lives.

As I live deeper into my eighties, I feel a softening of my edges, a blurring of rigidly held beliefs, an ability to see gradations of gray between the extremes of blacks and whites, a yielding of harsh judgments to more compassionate understanding. This is not to say that I no longer hold firm opinions, or that I have ceased to see the brilliant colors and intriguing shapes of the world around me, or that I now fail to be incensed by injustice and violence. I do not feel that I have become a paler version of my former self, diminished by my age, but rather that I have taken on more complexity, developed more nuance, enlarged my landscape of ideas, and that makes for a fuller, more variegated, and less sharp-edged personality. There is an interweaving of all aspects of the self, a blending of the threads of anger and sorrow and depression in with the brighter colors of love and joy and acceptance, producing a rich, more balanced, and more appealing life tapestry.

Facing the Abyss

It is quite likely that I will encounter major difficulties at some not-too-distant point, yet it is my hope that I may face these challenges with courage and acceptance, that I may become a good role model for my children, grandchildren, and great-grandchildren as well as for the other young men and women that I know and love. In accentuating the uplifting aspects, yet not losing sight of the inevitable constraints imposed by increasing age, I hope to help dispel much of the fear that so many young and middle-aged persons have of growing old. I hope to help demolish some of the more reprehensible stereotypes of the elderly by showing a more confident way, a more enriching and more fulfilling way, to live out our late years.

Recently I wrote a poem which is an expression of my own coming to terms with this phase of my long life. It is called "Facing the Abyss."

I stand, hesitant, knowing the abyss lies close ahead.
What, I wonder, is between me and that final plunge?
Will I slouch, staggering, eyes closed and head bowed?
Will I stumble and curse at my faltering step?
Will I arrogantly look away, denying what is before me?

Or will I stride forward assured, unblinking, unafraid?
Will I march to the steady beat of my own drum?
Will I step off the edge with head high and both eyes open?
Will my heart sing with joy as I fall into that vast
unknown?

I do not know.

But for now I walk with great care,
I look where I am going,
I keep open wide my eyes and heart,
Hoping that when I reach the rim,
I can step off that cliff
With full acceptance and confidence
And with no regrets.

~

Cousins, Norman. *Anatomy of an Illness as Perceived by the Patient.* New York: W. W. Norton, 1978.

O'Donohue, John. "For the Interim Time," *To Bless the Space Between Us: A Book of Blessings.* New York: Doubleday, 2008.

Roszak, Theodore. *America the Wise: The Longevity Revolution and the True Wealth of Nations.* Boston: Houghton Mifflin, 1998.

Scott-Maxwell, Florida. *The Measure of My Days.* New York: Penguin, 1968.

Weil, Andrew. *Healthy Aging: A Lifelong Guide to Your Physical and Spiritual Well-Being.* New York: Knopf, 2005.

Wise Elders and Old Fools

*I believe that as people grow older, they grow wiser—and
indeed want to grow wiser, as if to make good use of life's
final years.... [T]he true measure of wisdom is hope, and
hope is what the competence of elders brings to the
dilemmas of the young.*

Theodore Roszak
America the Wise

Wisdom and Folly

It has been said that old age represents a second childhood, implying not
just childishness but also a kind of foolishness. The opposite notion is
that as we age we develop knowledge, prudence, and insight, thus
becoming wise. That we are to be respected as wise elders or dismissed as
old fools seems to me a mistaken duality; the fact is that to be whole we
must concede qualities both wise and foolish. What might be useful to
examine is how those seemingly contradictory characteristics contribute
to the fullness of our lives. It surely will be to our advantage to imagine
ourselves as we grow into our old age as becoming wise elders *and* old
fools, or, perhaps more succinctly, aspiring to be defined by the
oxymoronic term *wise fools.*

The author-teacher-preacher Koholeth of the biblical book of Ecclesiastes
says that "The wise have eyes in their head, but fools walk in darkness.
Yet I perceived that the same fate befalls all of them." It is indeed wise to

have eyes in our head—and to keep them wide open—as we navigate the daylight of our lives. But since we must also traverse the treacherous terrain of the night, it is equally important that we embrace the foolhardy part of ourselves that dares to walk in darkness. In any stage of life, but especially as we grow old, learning to walk boldly through all shades of light and dark is an essential skill, for we are likely to encounter numerous bleak days and nights as we stumble or step without hesitation toward our final destination. The light of awareness and the darkness of uncertainty are both present as we travel this journey through life, just as both wisdom and folly are essential aspects of character if we are fully human.

Traditionally, wisdom is considered a characteristic of the elderly, requiring years of life experience to acquire, whereas foolishness, with its suggestion of impetuousness and thoughtlessness, is imputed to the young. In actuality both qualities can be found along the continuum of our lives; when we are young we frequently make wise decisions, and when old we often behave in decidedly foolish ways. Sometimes it is not clear what is wise and what is foolish. Paradox abounds.

The Fool

The archetype of the Fool is most famously represented, perhaps, in the Tarot, a deck of cards used for divinatory purposes in which each card has an image and a title exemplifying an archetypal concept. In the Rider-Waite deck the Fool is pictured as a young man, a stick with a bundle tied at the end swung over his right shoulder. In the other hand he holds a white rose, and at his feet is a small prancing dog. He is striding perilously close to the crumbling edge of a cliff, but he is not looking down to see what lies ahead.

The Fool of the Tarot suggests a kind of naive foolishness, an unbridled optimism that all will be well, for the young man, with no care or worry to impede his stride, is obviously unaware of, perhaps unconcerned by, the potential dangers that lie in front of him. He is on a journey, ready for adventure. He did have enough foresight to bring with him some essential belongings and his faithful animal companion. The white rose he carries is a sign of purity or innocence. The dog may represent his instinctual self.

Many of us at one point or another in our lives have lived the story of this figure. We have ventured out into something new, idealistically, foolishly, barely prepared, not knowing what awaits us, but with sufficient confidence—or hubris—to proceed, feeling assured that we will land safely and find our footing. Embarking on a new business venture, drastically changing our career direction, or entering into a new relationship can indicate our readiness for a fresh, possibly risky, but promising, new beginning. The Fool in us is ready to take a chance, to go forward, even though we cannot know what hazards may lie ahead.

I was a perfect example of the Fool when at age eighteen I ran away from home with a few summer clothes packed into a borrowed suitcase, no money, and no notion of where or how I would live when I reached my destination. I stepped off that metaphorical cliff and luckily landed without any serious mishap and have been grateful ever since for the courage I displayed in that youthful act of foolishness. I played that role again when I enrolled in graduate school for a doctorate at age sixty-nine, having little notion of the trials that I might encounter.

As we enter our later years all of us are fools in the sense that we are stepping off the edge of our early lives in order to explore new territory, that of elderhood, a place unknown and strange to us. We carry our bundle of essential goods (our experience and knowledge) over our shoulders, firmly grasp our optimism and hope symbolized by the white rose, and rely on our instincts to guide us through what may be a perilous future. We move forward, physically slowly but psychologically alert. As elders we are approaching the most awesome and mysterious chasm of all, our eventual death, but ideally we blithely and bravely continue, living life as fully as possible up to the very end. We hold tightly to that white flower of hope and stride into the unknown. By knowingly inhabiting this archetype, we demonstrate what it means to live our old age as wise fools.

The Court Jester

Another example of the Fool is the court jester who, according to Beatrice K. Otto in her book *Fools Are Everywhere*, is found to have existed throughout history and around the globe. The jester's behavior has fundamental similarities whether in the ancient courts of China or in medieval Europe. The primary characteristic of this kind of fool is that its humor is aimed at what we might call the establishment—kings and noblemen, pious ministers and priests, self-important scholars, corrupt or lazy government officials, anything or anyone deemed sacred. The court jester is irreverent, witty, clever, mischievous, and roguish.

One of the best-known examples in literature is the Fool in Shakespeare's *King Lear.* The king wishes to divide his kingdom among his daughters, but disinherits one who does not express her love for him in the way he prefers. Lear is tragically conflicted, and the Fool points out in a humorous way, using puns, riddles, and jokes, the foolishness of the King's attitudes and behavior. One example is when the Fool tells Lear, "Thou madest thy daughters thy mother: for…thou gavest them the rod and puttest down thine own breeches." When Lear asks, "Dost thou call me fool, boy?" the Fool replies, "All thy other titles thou hast given away; that thou was born with." The Fool's wisdom and insight delivered with clever and entertaining sayings allows him to exert profound influence over the king. One might say that in the witticisms of the Fool, wisdom is heard.

In today's world comedians such as Jon Stewart, Stephen Colbert, Trevor Noah, John Oliver, Samantha Bee, Sarah Silverman, Amy Schumer, and Bill Maher are our equivalent of court jesters. They use humor to point out the hypocrisies and contradictions in the words and behaviors of our political, civic, and religious leaders and media personalities. Just as famous jesters of Europe's courts were known throughout the kingdom for their jokes and jibes made at the expense of royalty, so today's comedians are celebrities for their keen insight into and revelations of the misadventures and misstatements of those in powerful positions.

We oldsters have a similar role to play in our society. Since for the most part we are not in positions requiring caution or discretion, we are no longer obligated to shelter the reputations of our leaders, whether in business, religion, or politics, nor do we find it necessary to defend our previously carefully regarded reputations by conforming to socially correct standards. Many of us in these late years awaken to the fact that we are now free to speak the truth as we see it, openly and candidly. We can dare to be truth-tellers, for we have little to lose by our honesty.

Adolph Guggenbühl-Craig, Jungian analyst and author, asserts that when we are old and no longer forced to make a living, we can then enjoy "the freedom of fools." We can waste time, do nothing if we like, ignore what goes on in the world, do things that are not reasonable or sensible, and thus relish a unique kind of existence not available when we were young. He reminds us that it can be dangerous to identify too strongly with the stereotype of elder wisdom lest we become overbearing, pompous, and unrealistic about what we know and what we have to offer. As he puts it, "The [wise] old fool rejects being regarded as intelligent and wise and refuses the projection of wisdom. This means that he rids himself of positions of power and frees himself from responsibility." We would do well to follow his advice, to not take ourselves too seriously, and to regularly engage in some foolishness.

Jung, though he frequently identified with the archetype of the wise old man, said, "I console myself with the thought that only a fool expects wisdom." We need not feel it necessary to present ourselves as "wise" old people who know what's best for everyone, but instead as we become stronger in our character and in our beliefs, we are unafraid to voice our opinions and to behave in ways that might to some seem foolish or inappropriate for our age. We can refuse to be reduced to the stereotypical wise elder while maintaining our integrity. We can claim the title of Wise Old Fool.

Wisdom

There is certainly a kind of wisdom to be found in some examples of the Fool, but just what is wisdom? Though volumes have been written about it, wisdom is notoriously difficult to define. One definition is "experience and knowledge together with the power of applying them critically or practically." Experience and knowledge are readily come by if one lives long enough, but how those are applied "critically or practically" seems crucial to our understanding of wisdom.

In our culture technical knowledge and information are held in particularly high regard; science is king and facts are paramount. Whereas the gathering, organizing, and distribution of data add to our store of knowledge and information and are skills necessary to function in the modern world, wisdom does not follow from those endeavors alone. The information and data must be integrated, utilized toward the accomplishment of worthy goals, applied in the broadest context, and used in ways that contribute to insight and understanding.

According to recent neurological research, the aging brain has a unique ability to do just that. Elkhonon Goldberg, neuroscientist and author of *The Wisdom Paradox: How Your Mind Can Grow Stronger as Your Brain Grows Older*, points out that the aging brain displays certain changes that are advantageous to the elderly and lead to what he calls wisdom. He reminds us that we must stop thinking of our aging minds in terms of losses only, for though we may lose some of our memory and our ability to sustain concentration, we nevertheless have much to gain. He describes the development over our lifetimes of pattern recognition, a facility which enables older adults to approach a broad range of unusual circumstances, issues, problems, and challenges as if they were familiar. We can do this because of our ability to recognize and utilize patterns similar to ones encountered in the past. In Goldberg's view this ability amounts to wisdom.

The gerontologist Gene Cohen similarly points out that older brains process information in a dramatically different way than younger brains. His research suggests that old people use both sides of the brain in an integrative manner to solve problems whereas young people tend to use primarily one side. He also says that making wise choices requires using both our logical and intuitive ways of processing information, drawing on both the right and left hemispheres, thereby utilizing the contributions of both the head and the heart. He says that there is some indication that as we age we rely on the left hemisphere more readily than when we are young.

Cohen emphasizes that continual personal development is another important key to cultivating wisdom. Wisdom, he writes, is "deep knowledge used for the highest good" thus adding to the word a moral component. He also emphasizes the role of our vast store of memory as fundamental to wisdom. When we are called upon to offer advice or to make wise decisions, we depend on our recollections of past actions and thoughts, both emotional and intellectual, which have been stored over our lifetimes. These memories are an essential resource for becoming wise elders.

Breadth and Depth

Recent advances in brain imaging techniques have made possible observing areas of the brain that correlate with various abilities, emotions, and states of mind. The findings of this research suggest that though older adults often have difficulty remembering specific bits of information, this is due largely to a gradually widening focus of attention that can diminish the ability to recall something like a name or a telephone number. More information is being taken in and processed in a way that makes it available later, thereby contributing to problem solving in a variety of circumstances. Along with the integration of both sides of the brain, the ability to assimilate data and apply it in a proper place and time is an indication of what might be called wisdom.

Just as there are archetypal images of the Fool, so we have the Wise Old Man or the Wise Old Woman. The particular image of the wise elder may vary depending on the culture, such as the honorary terms Grandmother and Grandfather often used in Native American societies, but its essence remains the same: an embodiment of the wisdom most evident in those who have lived long enough to accrue sufficient experience, knowledge, and insight to make them valuable members of their communities.

Theodore Roszak, in *America the Wise*, contends that one of the attributes of wisdom is the "ability to see through the illusions of youth." Such an outlook liberates us, "frees the mind and enlivens the soul." Furthermore, unlike many others, Roszak believes that wisdom is not a rarity, that as we grow older we automatically grow wiser because we elders truly wish to make good use of our final years. He insists that all we need do is examine our experience and take it seriously in order to offer wise and gentle criticism or words of encouragement to others, sharing our views and beliefs from what he calls a discriminating distance. If it is true, as Roszak writes, then *wisdom happens* and is everywhere around us.

A different point of view is offered by Dr. George E. Vaillant, director of the Landmark Harvard Study of Adult Development (mentioned in Chapter 1). He says, "To be wise about wisdom we need to accept that wisdom does—and wisdom does not—increase with age." His study indicates that though "Age facilitates a widening social radius and more balanced ways of coping with adversity, thus far no one can prove that wisdom is greater in old age." He also points out what seems obvious: wisdom is multifaceted and includes such qualities as maturity, common sense, moral discernment, appreciation of context, intelligence, and emotional intelligence. He also suggests that wisdom involves tolerance of ambiguity and paradox. As we age it becomes easier to accept uncertainty and not knowing. We learn that answers are not always definitive but often relative; we understand that life is filled with complexities and that there are many shades of gray.

Wisdom of the Heart

Ram Dass is a well-known spiritual leader (mentioned in Chapter 2) who has studied the practices of a variety of ancient wisdom traditions, including Hinduism, Zen Buddhism, as well as Sufi and Jewish mystical teachings. He insists that wisdom requires a spiritual dimension,

> the emptying and quieting of the mind, the application of the heart, and the alchemy of reason and feeling. In the wisdom mode, we're not processing information, analytically or sequentially. We're standing back and viewing the whole, discerning what matters and what does not, weighing the meaning and depth of things.

For those of us who have lived long, the "long view" has a strong resonance.

This vision of the spiritual aspects of aging values the development of wisdom over the mere accumulation of information, but as Ram Dass points out, "[T]he real treasure is being ignored: *wisdom is one of the few things in human life that does not diminish with age.*" From this perspective it is as wise elders that we are capable of and responsible for developing and sharing the kind of thinking and relating that our endangered world desperately needs if it is to survive. We can consciously foster within ourselves the qualities of sustainability, environmental sensitivity, regard for justice and fairness, patience, reflection, and, not least, a good sense of humor.

Though wisdom may be difficult to define, we seem to know it when we encounter it. Experience and knowledge are certainly necessary, as are perspectives and characteristics that enrich curiosity and creativity, foster relationships, and contribute to intellectual growth and emotional stability. Qualities associated with wisdom are authenticity, patience, compassion, kindness, humility, humor, playfulness, confidence, acceptance, awareness, serenity, and optimism. But it is the manner in which these traits are integrated and applied that is of primary importance. When we meet someone of advanced age who has intelligence, depth, compassion, a strong sense of self, an aura of calm and confidence, and who has not only benefited and learned from his or her life's experiences but is also motivated to share their insights, we feel in the presence of wisdom. Implicit in the concept is a sense of fairness, lack of harsh judgment, emotional balance, and genuine concern for others. Wisdom integrates all aspects of the developing self; it requires an ability to be still, to be reflective, to stand back and look at the whole without being caught up in minutiae. Wisdom is as much a way of being as a way of thinking or behaving. We must not forget, however, the importance of incorporating a measure of foolishness in with our wisdom so that we can truly grow into the admired status of being wise old fools.

$\sim$

Cohen, Gene. *The Mature Mind: The Positive Power of the Aging Brain.* Cambridge, MA: Basic Books, 2005.

Dass, Ram. *Still Here: Embracing Aging, Changing, and Dying.* Ed. Mark Matousek and Marlene Roeder. New York: Penguin, 2000.

Goldberg, Elkhonon. *The Wisdom Paradox: How Your Mind Can Grow Stronger as Your Brain Grows Older.* New York: Penguin, 2005.

Guggenbühl-Craig, Adolf. *The Old Fool and the Corruption of Myth.* Dallas: Spring Publications, 1991.

Jung, C. G. *Memories, Dreams, Reflections.* Ed. Aniela Jaffé. Trans. Richard and Clara Winston. New York: Vintage Books, 1989.

Otto, Beatrice K. *Fools Are Everywhere: The Court Jester Around the World.* Chicago: University of Chicago Press, 2001.

Roszak, Theodore. *America the Wise: The Longevity Revolution and the True Wealth of Nations.* Boston: Houghton Mifflin, 1998.

Vaillant, George E., M.D. *Aging Well: Surprising Guideposts to a Happier Life from the Landmark Harvard Study of Adult Development.* Boston: Little, Brown, 2002.

Death—The Elephant in the Room

We are so convinced that death is simply the end of a process that it does not ordinarily occur to us to conceive of death as a goal and a fulfillment, as we do without hesitation the aims and purposes of youthful life in its ascendance.

C. G. Jung
"The Soul and Death"

The Great Unknown

When I began writing this book on aging I had decided not to address the final event of our lives. But when I talked to friends about my decision they scolded me, saying I was tiptoeing around the elephant in the room, avoiding the very topic that is of greatest interest to those of us in the late stages of life. They were right, of course. Though we cannot know what it means to experience the cessation of our physical existence, we nevertheless are intensely curious about the profound mystery of death. For some that lack of knowledge engenders a deep-seated fear—fear of the unknown. We are haunted by questions: What does it feel like to be dying? What is it like to be dead? What happens after death? The fact is, we really do not know the answers, though some who have had near-death experiences feel they have glimpsed that enigmatic realm beyond our reality. Our lack of reliable information, however, does not preclude firm belief and/or endless speculation regarding what transpires after we take our last breath.

My reluctance to deal with this challenging subject was in part due to our cultural unease in discussing dying and death in an open and honest way. We tend to skirt the topic or use euphemisms such as "passing away," thus hoping to soften the fact of earthly finality. I hesitated also because of my own ambivalent feelings about the possibility, or promise, of an afterlife. There exists among many of us an enduring fascination with the notion of immortality, whether remaining in our earthly home or existing in some imagined (usually perfect) hereafter. In an effort to help overcome this fear of facing the end of life as we know it, we might benefit from hearing a few stories told by those nearing death and by studying reports from those who care for the dying. Many of these accounts are quite astonishing in their clarity and awareness of those final moments. We might also find comfort and reassurance by examining some of the beliefs and theories about immortality and the possible existence of life after death.

The Art of Dying

In medieval times there was a body of Christian literature the purpose of which was to provide guidance for the dying and for those attending them. One of these guides, called *Ars Moriendi*, or the "art of dying," instructed both the dying and their families about temptations to avoid, attitudes to adopt, and prayers to use. Presumably following these suggestions would lead to a "good death." A currently popular guide of this sort is *The Tibetan Book of Living and Dying*, in which suggestions are offered for ways to cultivate the spiritual attitudes and understanding that can help lead to a peaceful death. In a preface to the book the Dalai Lama offers this advice: "If we wish to die well, we must learn how to live well: Hoping for a peaceful death, we must cultivate peace in our mind, and in our way of life." All of us hope that our final days will be calm and orderly, undisturbed by pain or feelings of regret, but few of us know just how that can be achieved, how to equip ourselves to die a peaceful death.

Helen and Scott Nearing were among the early pioneers in the self-sufficiency movement, living a simple life in Maine, largely sustaining themselves with food grown on their organic Forest Farm. Helen Nearing gives us an account of her husband's dying experience, which she said was done with "deliberation and in full consciousness." Writing in her early nineties, she tells us that he was nearing one hundred when he announced at an evening meal, "I think I won't eat anymore." He felt his strength ebbing and had decided the time had come, as she said, "to call it quits." He drank fruit and vegetable juice for a month, then only water, and a week later, "He stepped quietly and consciously into death." One might say that Scott Nearing withdrew from life and drew into death.

Some individuals approach death with a sense of curiosity, like Marguerite Yourcenar, who wrote, "For my part, I would like to die fully conscious that I am dying...slow enough to allow death to insinuate itself into my body and fully unfold, so as not to miss the ultimate experience, the passage." Others may wish for a sudden, unexpected death, but only ten percent of deaths occur that way; ninety percent of us die slowly, following an extended period of disease-induced or age-related malaise. In spite of such forewarning, few of us have the foresight to articulate how we wish those last days to be spent. A serene passage like that of Scott Nearing, fully anticipated, carefully planned, and carried out with remarkable conscious awareness, is something we might all wish for, but it is rare indeed.

Perhaps it is our fear of death or our reluctance to discuss such matters that keeps many of us from sharing our thoughts about our final passage with those close to us. Numerous studies, many of which are reported in the surgeon Atul Gawande's book *Being Mortal*, have shown that having such conversations with our doctors and our families often can lead to a more peaceful process of dying. In some situations, however, for example Gawande's discussion of his father's death, no amount of planning fully prepares us for those final weeks, days, or hours. Unexpected medical crises or other factors can thwart our most careful arrangements.

Nevertheless, it can be helpful for all concerned to discuss our wishes with those close to us. It behooves us while we are still vital to give serious thought to just what we believe about death and dying, how we hope to face that inevitability, and how we wish to be cared for in our final days or months. Sharing those thoughts and preferences with family members and caretakers while we are still reasonably well and lucid is important, for there may come a time when we are no longer able to make our wishes known.

There have been some inspiring accounts from those close to death. Alice James, sister of Henry and William James, was fully rational and capable of sharing her thoughts and feelings before and during the dying process. She endured a prolonged illness, eventually succumbing to breast cancer. In 1891, nearing the end of her life, she wrote to William:

> It is the most supremely interesting moment in life, the only one, in fact, when living seems life, and I count it as the greatest good fortune to have these few months so full of interest and instruction in the knowledge of my approaching death. It is so simple to one's own person as any fact of nature, the fall of a leaf or the blooming of a rose, and I have a delicious consciousness, ever present, of wide spaces close at hand, and whisperings of release in the air.

Such a statement with its beautiful imagery—*whisperings of release*—is remarkable in its clarity and its courage. Whatever one's beliefs, such an open-hearted and open-minded acknowledgement of one's imminent demise is truly inspiring.

In February 2015, the renowned physician and author Oliver Sacks wrote an essay for *The New York Times* titled "My Own Life" in which he told of his recent diagnosis of multiple metastases of the liver. Now, he said, "I am face to face with dying." He told of seeing his life "as from a great altitude, as a sort of landscape, and with a deepening sense of the connection of all its parts. This does not mean I am finished with life." He went on to say that he felt "intensely alive" and that in the time that remained he wished "to deepen my friendships, to say farewell to those I love, to write more, to travel if I have the strength, to achieve new levels of understanding and insight."

Sacks also mentioned having "a sudden clear focus and perspective," indicating a measure of detachment. Nevertheless, he wrote, "I cannot pretend I am without fear. But my predominant feeling is one of gratitude. I have loved; I have been given much and I have given something in return...." He closed by saying that his life had been an enormous privilege and adventure, but even he, who did live an extraordinary life, was aware that facing our fears is a part of the process. Sacks died the following August, only a few months after he penned those words. His moving reflection on his imminent death provides us with an outstanding illustration of what it is like to live life fully and consciously up until the very end.

Some feel that acceptance of impending death grows out of belief in an afterlife. The Nearings, though not traditionally religious, believed that death did not involve a complete cessation of consciousness. As Helen states, birth and death are two events "in a whole life of livingness—with youth, maturity and old age, diversions in between—familiar features of human existence. Life links them all and continues beyond." There are many who firmly believe in the continued existence of the soul, certainly those whose religious beliefs assure them of an afterlife and also those who have had mystical or near-death experiences. There are as well those who have reached this belief through their study of science, finding some evidence that confirms for them the continued existence of consciousness in some form. Essentially, however, death remains a vast enigma, something we the living cannot truly comprehend. Nevertheless, we can deepen our understanding of the end of life by considering the perspectives of those who hold unusual views regarding death and others who have had some extraordinary experiences, including examples of my own.

Near-Death Visions and Dreams

Caretakers frequently report that some individuals who are nearing the end of life speak of family members who have preceded them in death standing by their bed and talking with them. Persons approaching those final hours sometimes seem to glimpse another world in which their loved ones are waiting for them, a world of peace and beauty. These accounts have been dismissed by some as hallucinations, but hospice nurses Maggie Callanan and Patricia Kelley, based on their extensive work with the dying, report that visual and verbal communications with the dead happen often and are significant; furthermore, these expressions offer caretakers and family members an opportunity to learn something from those facing imminent death. What may seem initially as confused, random talk can provide important clues to just what the dying person thinks or needs. For those of us who are witnesses to those near death, it is important to pay close attention to their moods, gestures, and utterances. By honoring their experiences we can assure them that they are not alone, that they are being heard, and thereby contribute to their peaceful passing.

Deathbed dreams are another source of information in the approach to the final stage of life. Even though accounts of such dreams have been written about for centuries, and psychologists and nurses frequently have made note of them, the medical establishment has tended to ignore such phenomena. As reported by Jan Hoffman in *The New York Times* in February 2016, however, a palliative care physician, Christopher W. Kerr, has researched the therapeutic role of end-of-life dreams and visions. The dream categories were "opportunities to engage with the deceased; loved ones 'waiting;' and unfinished business." Nearly all the patients reported dreams of love as well as dreams of incidents requiring resolution or forgiveness. Dreams of being greeted lovingly suggest the possibility of a more peaceful death. Sometimes there are dreams of preparing for a journey. Not long ago I dreamed that I was planning a trip but could not find my passport. Does this indicate that I really do not yet have everything that I need for my departure? Perhaps.

In a similar vein, I can report another quite astonishing personal experience. At age eighty-six I was in the hospital seriously ill following surgery for a ruptured appendix, when I appeared to one of my granddaughters who lived half a continent away. She described the event as a waking vision—a visit from me during which I discussed with her my death and what symbolic gift I wished to leave each member of my family, and how I wished my memorial service to be conducted, offering specific details about music, ritual, and food. She felt confident of my presence, saying that at the end of our conversation I lay down in bed with her, hugged her, and then departed "in a puff of air" out her bedroom window. Certain I had died, she was distraught, but what had been conveyed to her was so clear that she typed it out in three pages. I was heavily sedated at the time and unaware of this strange occurrence until I returned home several days later. When I read what she had written I was stunned at how accurately she had recorded my feelings and my wishes, all previously unknown to her. Reading her account today brings tears to my eyes. I am puzzled and awestruck at how this deeply personal information was transmitted. I wonder if I may have briefly died, or left my body somehow, but there is no medical evidence or scientific theory to explain what happened. In spite of the inscrutability of such an event, I feel strangely comforted and even more aware that both life and death are exceedingly mysterious.

Jung suggests that it is important for us to form some image of the hereafter, a myth about death and the land of the dead, even though we know that our conception may not be correct. Not to have done so, he says, is "a vital loss." He argues that reason is too limiting to satisfy our natural curiosity about death, for it can provide us with no certain answers. We must, therefore, be open to mythologizing, telling stories, and paying attention to the life of the unconscious that communicates with us through synchronicities, premonitions, and dreams. We may still have uncertainties, but we will be living in accordance with our instincts, not against them.

Several years ago I wrote my own fantasy of the afterlife, which I am aware has no validity from a rational perspective; nevertheless, it offers me some consolation. In my imaginary story I depart my body in a cloud-like manner, feeling myself expanding and then realizing that I am only one small part of a much larger entity. It is as if I am only one spoke of a huge wheel and that I am joined at the hub of the wheel to other aspects of my larger Self. I feel it will take a very long time to become acquainted with the immensity and variety of this expanded Self. There is also a sense that all that I have known, or done, or thought—good, bad, stupid, intelligent, kind, unkind—is encompassed in this entity. I know somehow that there is no judgment, that all events and behaviors are viewed with a deep, compassionate understanding and acceptance of the frailties of the human ego. I feel as if I am a cloud that separates, intersperses, and intermingles with other clouds of consciousness but can then reassemble into my own particular configuration. This ability to attract or blend with whatever or whomever I wish is astonishing, promoting feelings of great joy and delight.

There is a considerable amount of literature dealing with near-death experiences, as well as an organization, the International Association for Near-Death Studies (IANDS) that gathers information from those who have experienced what was presumably clinical death, then revived. The accounts have many things in common, most notably that the individuals are drawn toward a warm glowing light and feel an inexpressible sense of unconditional love. Frequently they are greeted by friends or family members who have died before them and often are presented with a nonjudgmental life review. These encounters have a profound effect on their ensuing lives, usually resulting in an enhanced and deepened spiritual outlook.

Here is one example of a near-death experience (NDE) offered by Lani Leary in her book *No One Has to Die Alone*:

> I suddenly had wisdom and a profound respect for the sacredness of all life, and I knew that there was not just one path by which to understand. This Spirit and loving presence that welcomed me home was larger, wiser, more compassionate and inclusive than any formal religion or word ascribed to it.... I realized that all my fear and grief had stemmed from an illusion of separation. This feeling of love, connection, and freedom was beyond what I ever dreamed possible.

Such experiences apparently do not happen to all persons in near-death situations but seem to leave a deep and lasting impression on those who have them.

In April 2015, *The Atlantic Magazine* published a lengthy article by Gideon Lichfield titled "The Science of Near-Death Experiences." Though the scientific evidence for NDEs has yet to be firmly established, the writer in his empirical investigation found many individuals whose experiences were so intense and so powerful that it did not matter to them whether what they saw and felt was due to some chemical reaction of their dying brains or was a glimpse of another reality. Their lives were changed dramatically as they discovered new purpose and meaning, which led to rethinking choices made in the past. As one person said, "My rational brain doesn't quite believe it but, having experienced it, I know it's true. So it's an ongoing discussion I'm having with myself." This comment reflects closely the feelings I have about my "appearance" to my granddaughter. I cannot explain it, but I do know that it has had a profound effect on me and members of my family.

The Natural Order

According to the late Sherwin Nuland, respected physician and author of *How We Die*, "Aging is not a disease. It is the condition upon which we have been given life. The aging and eventual death of each of us is as important to the ecosystem of our planet as is the changing of the seasons." That is, the natural cycle of life requires the death of the old in order to be replaced by the young and vigorous. The naturalness of death is echoed in these words of Thomas Cole: "Growing old and dying, like being born and growing up, will remain part of the cycle of organic life, part of the coming into being and passing away that make up the history of the universe." As Atul Gawande points out in his book *Being Mortal*, death "is not a failure. Death is normal. Death may be the enemy, but it is also the natural order of things."

In spite of being a natural, universal, and inevitable event, Nuland informs us that it is illegal everywhere in the world to write "old age" on a death certificate as the cause of death. A particular ailment or accident must be noted. Unfortunately, many in the medical profession seem to view death as failure, as all too often every possible procedure is recommended to avoid or prolong the time before that inescapable end. Giving the name of a disease to a natural process suggests that it can somehow be cured or thwarted. But Nuland states the obvious: "Old age is as insoluble as it is inevitable." And yet the medical profession trains practitioners to save lives by solving problems or untangling puzzles. If the problem cannot be solved or the puzzle deciphered, too often the attending physician loses interest in the patient.

Many doctors are more interested in trying to solve the riddle of disease and therefore prolonging life as long as possible than they are in recognizing the needs of an individual to die in the most comfortable and peaceful manner, even in the face of considerable financial and personal costs. Those doctors may see continued treatment as a way of offering hope, but sometimes the hope is empty and unjustified. As Gawande writes, "Our reluctance to honestly examine the experience of aging and dying has increased the harm we inflict on people and denied them the basic comforts they most need." Our modern medical approach has all too often focused on treatment without acknowledging the profound mystery of the passage called death.

The hospice movement offers an alternative to inappropriately aggressive medical measures. Hospice helps patients face the end of life by arranging for them to live their final days or months in comfortable and serene environments, as free of pain as possible, surrounded by those they love. Such sympathetic care addresses not only a patient's physical necessities but also emotional, social, and spiritual needs.

Palliative care provides seriously ill patients with relief from pain and stress. A study reported by Gawande found that terminally ill patients under the care of a palliative care physician stopped their chemotherapy sooner, entered hospice earlier, experienced less suffering, and, perhaps surprisingly, *lived 25 percent longer*. There apparently is some advantage in facing the reality of one's condition. As he says, "The lesson seems almost Zen: you live longer only when you stop trying to live longer." In addition to providing palliative care to the terminally ill, hospice workers are trained to support the families and caretakers of the dying. Many of us vastly prefer to die at home rather than in the chaos of the Intensive Care Unit or in the sterile environment of a hospital room. Hospice care can be arranged for persons in their homes or in nursing homes or other residential facilities where their special needs require professional care.

Ira Byock, physician and hospice director, has witnessed a broad range of behavior in his dying patients, some whose passing was tremendously painful with unaccountable suffering and others who found in those closing days or hours a deep sense of peace, even bliss. There is general agreement that one of the greatest fears of the dying is that they will be alone, so Byock writes that when his patients remain in relative comfort and know they will not be abandoned, they are often able to heal troubled relationships and strengthen the bonds of love, thus finding reconciliation and meaning in the final days of their lives.

Accordingly, though death can be difficult and stressful and accompanied by sorrow and grief, it can also bring comfort, closure, and completion. As Claire Leimback notes, "Death offers us so many opportunities, to reassess who we are and what we want from our own lives, to care for someone we love, to make last wishes come true, to be creative, to find laughter in the midst of sadness and to celebrate life." We would all wish to face the end of our lives with a sense that we have accomplished most of those goals.

The Question of Immortality

As firmly as some believe that there exists a continuation of our consciousness after physical death, there are others who hold the view, perhaps most eloquently expressed by the ancient Greek philosopher Epicurus, that we are mortal and that absolutely nothing, not the soul, not consciousness, survives once we die. It was his belief that death is total annihilation, the cessation of everything, the complete elimination of all experience. His argument is that we cannot experience death since there is no ego entity left to know what has occurred, so there should be no regrets and no fear. As he puts it, "While we are, death is not; when death is come, we are not. Death is thus of no concern either to the living or to the dead. For it is not with the living and the dead do not exist." For Epicurus, death is complete oblivion.

Though Epicurus did not deny the existence of gods, he felt they had no concern with the life of human beings other than serving as examples. His focus was on exhorting everyone to avoid pain and find maximum pleasure while alive. He was not recommending, as some believe, an extreme hedonism of excessive eating and drinking, but instead viewed pleasure as living a moderate, virtuous, and tranquil life. One way of avoiding pain was to vanquish the fear of death and instead to aspire to happiness by developing the virtues of courage, moderation, and prudence. His basic philosophy has influenced many current thinkers, especially atheists, who do not believe in an afterlife.

There are others whose desires or beliefs serve as an interesting contrast to the Epicurean philosophy in that they wish to live forever in this world or in an imagined afterlife. Immortality is something humans have thought about and sought throughout the ages, desperately hoping to find some magical elixir that would prolong their lives indefinitely. According to contemporary philosopher Stephen Cave, such a desire for immortality, as unrealistic as it may be, has served us well, for it is "the foundation of human achievement; it is the wellspring of religion, the muse of philosophy, the architect of our cities and the impulse behind the art. It is embedded in our very nature and its result is what we know as civilization." He sees the goal of immortality as a universal impetus to our worldly accomplishments.

Cave mentions four narrative paths that promise immortality: *Staying Alive*, the *Resurrection Narrative*, the *Soul Narrative*, and *Legacy*. There are countless stories of leaders and adventurers looking for some potion that guarantees eternal life. Though our life span is increasing due to more sanitary living conditions and medical advances, there is no indication that such a brew is likely to be found. Nevertheless, there are numerous ongoing research studies seeking to find the ultimate cause of aging and death with, perhaps, an expectation that just maybe life can be extended indefinitely. The question is, in what state would our bodies be? The thought of remaining forever young and inexperienced seems unfulfilling, yet an unending prolongation of decline and decay seems horrifying.

The next path, the *Resurrection Narrative*, provides hope for eternal life even if we cannot live forever on this planet in our current bodies. Each of the three monotheistic religions teaches some version of life after death. Followers of these traditions believe they will be revived in something like Heaven (or perhaps Hell). In the Christian tradition there are differing opinions among theologians regarding bodily resurrection as opposed to continuing as disembodied spirits or souls. Unlike Christianity, in which life after death is an important theological component, the topic is not central to Judaism; there are no definitive doctrines regarding afterlife in the Torah, though various possibilities have been raised over the centuries. Islam teaches that at the Day of Reckoning Muslims will face judgment and go to either Heaven or Hell.

Another example of the resurrection narrative is the Hindu concept of reincarnation in which the spirit or soul of a deceased person begins a new life in another body. Deepak Chopra, writing about life after death, describes an astral plane, wherein it is determined that reincarnation occurs at a higher soul level than the one lived previously on earth. He feels that the soul's motivation for returning to an earthly existence is "to fulfill desires and to rejoin with familiar souls." Chopra lists the themes that represent his thinking regarding the afterlife: It is a place of newfound clarity. It isn't static, for we continue to evolve and grow after we die. Furthermore, choice doesn't end with death; it expands. And finally, as before death, after death we tend to see what our culture has conditioned us to see, but eventually the soul makes creative leaps that open new worlds. Chopra observes that an old culture like India "makes room for love and death together, not as enemies but as entwined aspects of one life."

The list of strategies for attaining immortality via resurrection would not be complete without the mention of cryonics, a modern method in which the cadaver, or sometimes just the head, is frozen in the assumption that the body will be rejuvenated, cured of all disease, at some point in the future when the problems of illness and death have been solved. A more up-to-date version envisions uploading ourselves onto our computers and, after some alterations or corrections, downloading ourselves into new bodies—avatars of sorts.

The third path of attaining immortality is that of the *Soul Narrative*, surviving as a spiritual entity, or soul. There is anecdotal evidence for such existence from reports of near-death or mystical experiences, quite convincing paranormal incidents and remarkable dreams involving those who have died or are about to die. I have been witness to occasions when there was facilitated communication "between the realms." There is no way to authenticate such exchanges, but I have found many of them quite persuasive. Whether or not these are "souls" or spiritual beings making connection with the living is beyond our rational understanding.

There remains the path of *Legacy*, something that most of us understand as a way of not just bequeathing our worldly goods but also leaving behind our values or beliefs or accomplishments; those too may represent a kind of immortality. Some of us have children, and all of us know persons on whom we have had a significant impact. But even these aspects of ourselves are destined to vanish at some point, for those people will die and all that we left behind will eventually fade away and be forgotten.

Cave's solution to the immortality quest is what he calls the *Wisdom Narrative*. He sees our predicament as our desire to live forever on this earth even though we know that fulfilling such a yearning would be disastrous. It is hard to imagine how we would avoid becoming numb with boredom after a few centuries of life. "We need finitude to give life value, yet that finitude comes packaged with the fear of death…. Wisdom, therefore, mean[s] finding a way to accept and live with mortality." Beyond that he suggests that we cultivate selflessness, or an ability to identify with others, that we maintain a sense of gratitude, and that we learn to live more in the moment. This narrative, Cave says, "is a powerful alternative…, one that balances a positive love of life with managing the fear of that life's end and by focusing our attention on the here and now and on the world outside of the self…." By following these recommendations, we can help "make the one life we have a better, richer, more meaningful one." This certainly seems a worthwhile endeavor.

Andrew Solomon, writing in *The New York Times*, adds another dimension to the wisdom narrative. He says that knowledge of our mortality enhances our desire for closeness. He suggests that if his 88-year-old father and he were to live forever, their relationship would not be the same, for its "affection would be stripped of its poignancy and urgency." The same is true of his feeling for his children, since if they were to remain at their young ages, he "wouldn't cling to their childhood for its sweetness; nor...endure its liabilities with the reassurance of imminent maturity." And then he makes this thought-provoking statement: "The cornerstone of optimism is the willingness to believe that the inevitable is desirable." For him, "There is no other fruitful point of view." If we were convinced that death is not only inevitable but desirable we would be freed from much of our fear.

Intentional Exodus

Writing about death cannot be complete without addressing the controversial subject of physician-assisted suicide, sometimes referred to as death with dignity or aid in dying. Many people feel strongly about having some control over their time of death, asserting that they have every right to determine when they can no longer tolerate the pain or circumstances of terminal illness. One argument put forth by the ACLU for the Right to Die movement states, "The right of a competent, terminally ill person to avoid excruciating pain and embrace a timely and dignified death bears the sanction of history and is implicit in the concept of ordered liberty." There appears to be a growing number of persons who feel they have a right to die with dignity under circumstances and timing of their choosing. Currently in the United States, certain kinds of physician-assisted death are legal in Oregon, Washington, Vermont, California, Colorado, and Montana, and laws are pending in other states.

Eligibility for aid in dying in the United States, based largely on the Oregon Death with Dignity Act enacted in 1997, requires that the person be terminally ill with the expectation of death within six months, a resident of the state, able to make decisions for him/herself, eighteen years old or older, and two physicians must verify that these conditions have been met. Also the person must be able to administer the medication themselves. In some countries in Europe, especially the Netherlands and Belgium, the requirements are much less stringent. People who are experiencing "unbearable suffering with no prospect of improvement" qualify for physician-assisted suicide, and the physician may deliver the fatal injection. Assisted dying is available for children over twelve with parental consent. In Belgium there are no minimum age limits, though the child must be close to death and in great pain. Those with severe mental anguish or intolerable psychological pain (as opposed to physical pain) may also request assistance to die.

Those who oppose such laws, particularly some disability activists, use the slippery slope argument, believing that assisted dying might eventually be applied to disabled people and will inevitably lead to other forms of euthanasia for any group devalued by society. There is the fear, for example, that mentally disabled patients or the elderly who have no advocates might be considered useless, or a family might decide that a member is too expensive to care for. If a person is not competent, has advanced Alzheimer's, for example—what then? Could someone else, perhaps a doctor, make the decision that that life is no longer tolerable? Might this lead to misuse of the right? There is also the question of whether persons with psychological illness such as severe depression or suffering from unbearable grief are mentally competent to make such a fatal decision. Who has the right to decide?

Another group that is vehemently opposed to Right to Die legislation is the Catholic church and groups loosely affiliated with it. Catholic hospitals are not obligated to follow advance directives such as Do Not Resuscitate if they are contrary to Catholic teaching. Partly this conflict is due to the change in our definition of death. It used to be based on the absence of heartbeat, but with new measures for resuscitation and the use of ventilators, the heart can be kept going long after the brain has ceased to function. In a famous case, Terri Schiavo was kept "alive" in a persistent vegetative state for fifteen years before the courts finally agreed to allow her feeding tube to be removed.

Philosophical, ethical, and practical complications arise from these differing perspectives. It is not difficult to empathize with the desire of a person with a terminal illness and intractable pain to wish for the right to die before losing all dignity, all pleasure, all essence of what it means to be alive. It is also possible to understand how those immersed in deep depression, despair, and hopelessness and see no purpose in prolonging their torment make the profoundly tragic decision to end their lives. Of course the latter is not an acceptable reason for physician-assisted death in the United States since depression is not a terminal illness.

More difficult to grasp is the action of someone like Carolyn Heilbrun, retired professor at Columbia University, author of numerous books, and tireless promoter of feminist scholarship, who at age seventy-seven decided to end her life after going for a weekly walk with a very good friend. She was in good health, seemingly enjoying a happy marriage, with children and grandchildren, but she went home and took her life, apparently following instructions from what was then the Hemlock Society. She left a note that said, "The journey is over. Love to all." She had written about her intention, saying she did not wish to ever be a burden. Her son is quoted as saying that "she wanted to control her destiny, and she felt her life was a journey that had concluded."

Perhaps some see Heilbrun's decision as an act of courage, but others might see it from a different angle. It appears that she was so frightened of becoming dependent—"useless," as she put it—that she denied herself the experience of accepting help from others and deprived her family and friends the opportunity of being with her through one of life's most profound passages. I am reminded of William Styron's words when he was in the depths of a severe clinical depression, what he called "despair beyond despair," and had decided to kill himself. He heard the beautiful Brahms *Alto Rhapsody* which pierced his heart "like a dagger" and brought to mind all the joys he had known in his home—the children, the work, the pets. It was, he said, "more than I could ever abandon.... And just as powerfully I realized I could not commit this desecration on myself." He was not well, for he was admitted to the hospital the next day, but his decision to choose life over death must have come about due to a transcendent experience brought about by the music. And it must have been a huge relief to his family and friends.

Facing the End

One of the earliest pioneers in the field of thanatology (the scientific study of death and dying) was Elizabeth Kübler-Ross, a psychiatrist who worked with terminally ill patients. In her groundbreaking book *On Death and Dying*, published in 1969, she described five steps in the dying process: *denial*, when patients cannot accept the reality of impending death; *anger*, when feelings of resentment, even rage, bring on the question, "Why me?"; *bargaining*, which elicits the desire for some sort of agreement with God or others to postpone the inevitable; *depression*, when patients can no longer deny their condition and become despondent; and finally *acceptance*, when the dying can contemplate their death with some degree of quiet expectation. Though Kübler-Ross wrote that not all patients experienced these emotional states, and not all in this order, her work has been questioned by subsequent research. What is most significant, however, is that she opened a dialogue about dying, a subject that previously had been largely ignored.

It seems inevitable, and appropriate, that each of us will face our final days in our own way. My husband, who had lived with increasing cognitive loss due to Alzheimer's disease for more than ten years, fortunately had a very peaceful ending. He had been in hospice care twice, the first time when he still had some degree of lucidity. The hospice nurse and I often talked with him about death, and he spoke openly of what he imagined would happen. Though thoroughly committed to science, he believed firmly that his consciousness would continue to exist, and he spoke frequently about his excitement at the prospect of exchanging ideas in his bodiless state with David Bohm, a physicist for whom he had great respect. He expressed no anxiety, fear, or regrets.

When after a few months his condition improved to the extent that he was removed from hospice, I asked what had happened, since he had seemed so prepared and even eager for death. His reply: "Death is much more complicated than I thought." About a year later I arrived for my regular visit to his residential care facility and could see immediately that something had changed in his look and demeanor. When I asked what was happening, he replied, "You really don't want to know." I knew then that he was preparing to die. He refused all food and drink, slipped into a coma, and died five days later. Those days gave us time as a family to gather around him, talk to him, sing to him, tell him that we loved him. One evening, when the time seemed near, we gathered in a circle around his bed, saying our goodbyes. I sang "Let Me Call You Sweetheart," and as I leaned over his bed to kiss him, his lips puckered in response. Our final interaction was sweet and loving, and he did indeed die later that night. I had grieved for years over the gradual loss of my husband of almost sixty years, but his dying time was so serene, so beautiful, that what I felt was a kind of joy when he finally left behind the body that no longer served him well.

The Well-Planned Exit

We can try to ensure that our dying time is to some degree in accordance with our wishes, by signing a living will and/or other directives and by having open and honest discussions with our doctor and family members, as described earlier. That requires us, while we are still able, to think about our preferences regarding our care at the end of life. Such conversations might focus on what we value, whether we wish to prolong life as long as possible, including the use of heroic measures, or to withdraw from treatment in order to die at home or in a hospice facility. We might explore the notion of physician-assisted death if it is legally available. We might discuss how and with whom we would like to spend our last moments.

On my desktop computer is a folder titled "Death Info" that contains suggestions for my memorial service and burial, along with some poems and music that I like; information for an obituary; financial information; a document called Five Wishes, which has to do with end of life care; my afterlife fantasy; a Values History that is somewhat similar to the Five Wishes; and an Ethical Will, which is a document written for family and friends that records my significant beliefs, hopes, moral and ethical imperatives, disappointments, and accomplishments. I included reflections regarding what I would like my legacy to be in the following areas: Relationships, Education, Social Responsibility and Politics, Spiritual Pursuits and Inner Work, Friendships, and Creativity. The Ethical Will concludes with the following list of the things I consider important:

- To continue to learn and to be open to new ideas.

- To make new friends of all ages at all stages of life.

- To maintain meaningful relationships, which requires time, attention, and effort.

- To do inner work—through therapy, dream-work, meditation, or by any means appropriate and helpful.

- To be open to mystery and not-knowing.

- To develop self-awareness.

- To have some means of creative expression.

- To take responsibility for one's behavior.

- To view each challenge in life as an opportunity for spiritual growth.

- To develop compassionate understanding, simple kindness, for all humans, including one's self.

- To be discerning enough to know the difference between what is good and what is not.

- To develop a sense of humor and to laugh whenever possible.

- To be authentic, sincere, and honest, true to one's self.

- To not be afraid of failure for it is a source of learning.

- To be generous.

- To ask for forgiveness from those we have hurt and offer forgiveness to those who have hurt us.

- To frequently express gratitude to family and friends.

- To express love for others and accept their love in return.

Those of us who are witnessing the dying of a loved one may also have some important things to say while there is still time. All too often we wait until it is too late to convey our deepest feelings to those we care for most. Common suggestions for what to communicate are the following: I love you. Thank you. Please forgive me. I forgive you. It's okay to go.

I would add to that the paramount value of developing and expressing a sense of gratitude, for that is what brings us the most joy and happiness. That sense of deep appreciation of a life fully lived is frequently stated by those nearing death. Perhaps as we approach our final days we are more thankful than ever for the extraordinary gift of life. Being aware of the nearness of death offers opportunities to examine our lives, to acknowledge our good deeds, to admit our failures, to recognize the influence we have had on others, to fulfill our last wishes and desires, to express our love for family and friends, and to find ways to laugh and celebrate life. We can also set an example for others by facing death with courage, accepting Solomon's belief that the "inevitable is desirable."

I like the comment of Jungian analyst Adolph Guggenbühl-Craig on accepting our ambivalence about death. He says, "The most courageous way to die is to be aware of all the contradictory feelings, to experience them fully, to tremble with fear, and to tremble with longing and expectation. Then one will know the bitterness and sweetness of death fully." Another bit of advice is offered by Stephen Levine in his book *A Year to Live*: "We prepare for death by living every second, living life minutely, exploring our body and mind with a merciful awareness." Being mercifully aware of both our fear and our longing will serve us well as we move into death.

Nuland maintains that if we can become attuned to an evolving perspective that recognizes the realities of our past, present, and future, then we can attain in our ending time a formerly unknown and unexpected serenity. This process, he says, "begins with an acknowledgement that the evening of life is approaching. But with that approach comes foreseeable possibilities.… It is incumbent on each of us to cultivate his or her own wisdom." Facing death with serenity and equilibrium is perhaps what we strive for most.

There are many who have an unshakable faith that some essence of ourselves continues on after our all-too-brief interlude here on earth, that consciousness or the soul is never extinguished. Others are equally certain that death is the total extinction of our physical and mental being. Either way, just what may happen after our limited lifetime is beyond our knowing. My thought is that if there is nothingness after death, then I have nothing to fear, but if there is another world offering new adventures and opportunities for growth, then I would rejoice in that marvelous discovery. In either case what we do know, and have some measure of control over, is how we prepare to face the cessation of life as we know it.

A beautiful passage from the Jewish *Gates of Prayer* can well serve us as we live out our years, months, or days before our time has come to depart this earth:

> Let us treasure the time we have,
> and resolve to use it well,
> counting each moment precious—
> a chance to apprehend some truth,
> to experience some beauty, to conquer some evil,
> to relieve some suffering, to love and be loved,
> to achieve something of lasting worth.

～

Byock, Ira. *Dying Well: The Prospect for Growth at the End of Life.* New York: Riverhead Books, 1997.

Callanan, Maggie, and Patricia Kelley. *Final Gifts: Understanding the Special Awareness, Needs, and Communications of the Dying.* New York: Bantam Books, 1992.

Cave, Stephen. *Immortality: The Quest to Live Forever and How It Drives Civilization.* New York: Crown, 2012.

Chopra, Deepak. *Life After Death: The Burden of Proof.* New York: Harmony Books, 2006.

Cole, Thomas R. *The Journey of Life: A Cultural History of Aging in America.* Cambridge: Cambridge University Press, 1992.

Dalai Lama. Foreword, in Sogyal Rinpoche, *The Tibetan Book of Living and Dying.* New York: HarperCollins, 1992.

Epicurus. *The Epicurean Philosophers.* Trans. John Gaskin. Everyman, 1995.

Gates of Prayer: The New Union Prayer Book. New York: Central Conference of American Rabbis Press, 1975.

Gawande, Atul. *Being Mortal: Medicine and What Matters in the End.* New York: Henry Holt, 2014.

Grigoriadis, Vanessa. "A Death of One's Own" [on Carolyn Heilbrun's suicide]. *New York Magazine,* December 8, 2003.

Guggenbühl-Craig, Adolf. *The Old Fool and the Corruption of Myth.* Dallas: Spring Publications, 1991.

Hoffman, Jan. "A New Vision for Dreams of the Dying." *The New York Times.* February 2, 2016.

James, Alice. *The Death and Letters of Alice James.* Ed. Ruth Bernard Yeazell. Exact Change, 1981.

Jung, C. G. *Memories, Dreams, Reflections.* Rev. ed. Recorded and edited by Aniela Jaffé. Trans. By Richard and Clara Winston. New York: Vintage Books, 1989.

Jung, C. G. "The Soul and Death," in *Jung on Death and Immortality.* Selected by Jenny Yates. Princeton, NJ: Princeton University Press, 1999.

Kübler-Ross, Elisabeth. *On Death and Dying.* New York: Scribner, 1969.

Leary, Lani, *No One Has to Die Alone: Preparing for a Meaningful Death.* New York: Atria, 2012.

Leimbach, Clare, Trypheyna McShane and Zenith Virago. *The Intimacy of Death and Dying.* Crows Nest, Australia: Allen & Unwin, 2009.

Levine, Stephen. *A Year to Live: How to Live This Year as if It Were Your Last.* New York: Bell Tower, 1997.

Lichfield, Gideon. "The Science of Near-Death Experiences: Empirically investigating brushes with the afterlife." *The Atlantic Magazine.* April 2015.

Nearing, Helen. *Light on Aging and Dying.* New York: Harcourt Brace, 1995.

Nuland, Sherwin B. *How We Die: Reflections on Life's Final Chapter.* New York: Knopf, 1994.

Sacks, Oliver. "My Own Life." *New York Times.* February 19, 2015.

Solomon, Andrew. "Life Is for the Dying." *New York Times Book Review.* February 14, 2016.

Styron, William. *Darkness Visible: A Memoir of Madness.* New York: Vintage Books, 1990.

Yourcenar, Marguerite. *With Open Eyes: Conversations with Matthieu Galey.* Trans. Arthur Goldhammer. Boston: Beacon, 1984

Epilogue: The Privilege of Growing Old

So we'll live, and pray and sing,
and tell old tales, and laugh
At gilded butterflies...
And take upon us the mystery of things
As if we were God's spies.

William Shakespeare
King Lear

Growing into advanced old age is awesome, mystifying, humbling—and often exasperating, exhausting, and frightening. When I began this journey so very long ago I had no idea what might happen to me, what directions I might take or decisions I might make. As I come closer to the end I look back in amazement at all the ups and downs I have survived, suffered with, and benefited from: joy, sorrow, despair, bliss, misery, love, illness, grief, success, failure—all of which have contributed to my humanness. Living long has allowed me the opportunity to forge a deeper understanding of and greater insight into the significance and consequences of all the fortunes and misfortunes that have been a part of my life.

As noted in earlier chapters, the usual expectation as we grow old is that our world will shrink, our contacts become limited, our activities restricted, and our intellectual and social horizons narrowed. It is thought that we will largely withdraw from society and become focused on ourselves, especially on our physical health. In many respects that is what happens. At the same time, however, I have found myself broadened and deepened as I have become more heedful of my interior life. I have become more aware of and appreciative of everyday pleasures, those simple comforts and delights that I once ignored or took for granted. I have also learned to value my relationships ever more deeply. The degree to which I have shifted my attention towards those positive mental, psychological, and spiritual viewpoints has contributed enormously to my sense of overall well-being.

This kind of inner work (discussed in detail in Chapter 5) requires thinking seriously about our beliefs, our values, and our behavior, while continuing to question or affirm our religious or spiritual practices. We may begin to pay less attention to worldly events and concentrate more fully on our dreams, fantasies, and thoughts about living and dying. This internal aspect of the self might be referred to as *soul*, something that seems to be different from yet intimately connected to our physical bodies. Immersing ourselves in soulful meditation and contemplation helps us make meaning of our lifetime of experiences and relationships, permits the free range of our imagination, encourages us to acknowledge the importance of love, and allows us to more readily accept the reality of death.

When we pay close attention to our memories and musings, we often become aware that there are things of greater concern than material goods or external reality. This change in perspective permits a spaciousness to develop within the psyche, making room for new attitudes and allowing for receptiveness to whatever this stage of life offers us. Such expansion clarifies our vision, deepens our spirit, and opens our hearts. We become less judgmental and more compassionate; we understand the paradoxes, complexities, and subtleties that govern our lives and are less likely to see circumstances in terms of extremes.

As we are emotionally released from old bindings we experience a new kind of freedom; though in some ways our horizons may contract, in other ways they are expanded. Our sure knowledge that our time is finite helps focus our attention on what and who is most important to us, thus opening our hearts to a wide range of possibilities. One possibility is forming new friendships in our late years. Like my oldest friends, my newest friends—several made in the last five years—provide me with much love and respect, thus helping continue to broaden and deepen me. They play an enormous role in reflecting back to me some of my better qualities, thus supporting my desire to remain compassionate with myself and others. I cherish those relationships, for I could not be the person I am today without their presence in my life.

So often we forget that it is indeed a blessing to be old. We all know tragic stories of those whose lives ended much too early—children, young people, mothers or fathers of young children, some of them members of our families whose loss we shall always grieve. As I acknowledge those premature deaths, I am reminded of my own good fortune. Along with appreciation for my old age has come serenity, contentment, and a sense of completion, of having reached an acceptance of where my life's path has taken me. There comes great joy in just *being*, without feeling a need to accomplish anything. There is a sense of release, of a weight lifted from my shoulders, and of deep pleasure in and gratitude for just *being alive*. So those of us who have had the advantage of longevity must never forget how blessed we are to be members of the clan of elders.

Now that I am close to being among the *oldest old* I think about all I have learned throughout my life and especially what I have experienced since the age of sixty. I am astonished—and aghast to think all I would have missed had I not lived this long. I have awakened to the miracle of being alive. By living long I have had the opportunity to witness a great span of history. I can look back almost a century, recall ordinary and extraordinary events, both personal and global. To mention only a few: I know what it is to grow up and work on a cotton and tobacco farm in the South during the Great Depression in a house with no electricity or running water, to remember the sorrows and grief caused by the gross injustices of legalized racial segregation, to live through World War II and later the contentious Vietnam War, the Iraq wars, as well as current upheavals in the Middle East, to suffer the anxieties of adolescence, to run away from home to marry the man I loved, to know the passion of desire and marriage, to meet the challenges of college and graduate school, to give birth to children, to experience the darkness of depression, to recover from that terrible feeling of despair, to suffer and recuperate from illness, to create things of practical value and beauty, to develop genuine friendships with my adult grandchildren and other young people, to know the immense joy of watching granddaughters become loving mothers, and thereby becoming a great-grandmother.

Though I am on familiar terms with despair and grief, I have also experienced incredible moments of grace, when the universe seems perfect just as it is, when my life is beautiful and bountiful beyond compare, when I feel worthy and appreciated, when I am overflowing with peace and joy, when the panorama of my experiences spreads out before me, full and rich and many-colored. I know what it is to love and be loved, to work, to play, to laugh, to cry, to nurture a family, to explore and heal many of my psychological conflicts and needs, to form deep and meaningful friendships, and yes, to grieve over the deaths of some I love. I am in awe when I reflect on the vast array of experiences I have had during my long life span.

I see the arc of my life as a slow unfolding of my authentic personhood, especially in my later years. I look back on my early behavior as a fumbling effort to nurture that fragile, seeking, struggling seedling self, and that endeavor continues into my old age, trying to be patient and compassionate with my failures. I am still exploring, still observing, and still learning from the course of my own maturation, with all its encumbrances and supports, pains and pleasures. Just as a plant grows in response to water, sunlight, and nutrients in the soil, so I have unfolded in response to my life experiences and to all who have been a part of my story. So, at this late stage of aging, I have a profound sense of gratitude for that mysterious life force or destiny that has guided me thus far. There is now an intensity, a heightened sensitivity, and a deepened appreciation for the gift of life itself.

At this late stage of my life everything has an added poignancy. Tears come more easily. My heart seems to have a softness and tenderness not present in my earlier years. I am deeply touched by seemingly trivial things, such as witnessing small acts of kindness whether to myself or others, sitting in my garden absorbing the essence of the beautiful flowers and plants, returning a smile from a stranger at the grocery store, or saying goodbye to a friend after a lunch at which we shared intimate details of our lives. These simple occasions now seem profound to me.

It is as if I am more alive than ever before. I am extraordinarily fortunate, for I feel infused with unexpected vigor and vitality, giving me an unparalleled sense of well-being. As I live through my final time upon this beautiful imperiled earth, I rejoice in the life I have lived; it has been a marvelous, fulfilling adventure, one I could never have imagined. What a privilege it is to grow old!

∼

Leah Friedman, Ph.D.

After an early career as an audiologist, Leah dedicated herself to marriage and family before becoming in midlife a still-life photographer exploring symbolic imagery of the unconscious. These images led to a deep interest in Jungian psychology. At age 69 she entered a doctoral program in Mythological Studies at Pacifica Graduate Institute—she was the oldest student in her class—and received her degree at age 73. Leah's experience in developing and conducting rituals is recounted in her book, *The Power of Ritual*. She has also written a memoir, *Leafings & Branchings*.

Made in the USA
San Bernardino, CA
12 November 2017